Little Books of Guidance

Finding answers to life's big questions!

Also in the series:

PATRICIA M. LYONS

What Is Evangelism?

CHURCH
PUBLISHING
INCORPORATED

A little
book of
guidance

Church Publishing
19 East 34th Street
New York, NY 10016
www.churchpublishing.org

Cover design by Jennifer Kopec
Typeset by Denise Hoff

A record of this book is available from the Library of Congress.

ISBN-13: 9781640652125 (pbk.)
ISBN-13: 9781640652132 (ebook)

Printed in Canada

Contents

Introduction: From Burden to Broadcast to Blessing

Evangelism is listening.

This liberating and life-giving fact is contrary to so many of the messages about Christianity going back to at least the fourth century. Roman Emperor Constantine acknowledged the profound proliferation and political power of the followers of Jesus and named Christianity the mandated religion of the Empire. At that time and long after, Christianity was forced upon people by law and by sword. However, sacred and faithful evangelism—contrary to the habits and sins of any Empire—is not primarily an act of speaking or manipulating or even persuading.

Evangelism is first and foremost the ministry of the Holy Spirit in the world. In the beautiful image of creation found in Genesis, the world began with the Holy Spirit breathing and blowing over the whole earth, blessing, sustaining, and transforming chaos into creation, darkness into light, and void into life. Evangelism is what the Holy Spirit is doing, ever arriving as the catalytic and contagious Good News of God's love. Although all creatures are invited to experience, embrace, and expand the love of God, evangelism is chiefly the holy work of God to make God known throughout all creation. To put it more directly, evangelism is what God does and what God is ever doing at every moment and every place and in every heart. The Holy Spirit is a siren sounding, even now, to find and follow the love of God.

The first step of human evangelism is to listen for the Spirit's invitation to join God in loving the world and in loving yourself.

The Holy Spirit evangelizes us, bringing the Good News of God into our lives. Some people listen to God in silent prayer, asking God to speak. Others listen for God in community or ritual, hearing God in scripture and song. Still others listen for God in human relationships, hearing God's hope and healing in the wounds or wonders of other people. When we begin to listen for God (and not just talk or sing at God), we experience God's constant evangelism of everything, drawing all that is toward the new heaven and the new earth. Creation is an act of God's evangelism.

Today's Reality

For centuries, Christians have spoken of their burden to convert the world. Although many generations of faithful people wanting holiness have participated in this burden of converting and done so with sincerity and love, I am glad that we in the Episcopal Church have moved away from this paradigm of colonizing the world with Christianity. Though the gospel was often shared and embraced by people who have made Christianity their own, the colonial conversion model has also come with moral disasters, war crimes, and cultural failures. Those who interpreted (and continue to interpret) the Great Commission as permission to subdue the earth with Christianity have driven as many people away from Christ as toward him. The increasing pluralism of America in recent decades has exposed the shallowness and arrogance of this model.

The twentieth century in America brought a crisis of membership in organized religion. And that century continues to leave us in difficult times. It is hard to describe the present and the future of the post-institutional and post-Christian century that we are living. So many institutions in the public square are collapsing.

Membership trends for every kind of voluntary association in America are going downward, everything from the Rotary Club to bowling leagues to bingo nights. There appears to be a decline in organized association or religion of any kind.

In fact, statistics[1] tell us that the whole globe is experiencing a decline in the participation in any religion at all. At the same time, extremist groups, perhaps fueled by the anxieties and fear that come from this global decline of religion, have taken up vitriol and violence against neighbors or migrants, making it even harder for people who are not religious to take the whole enterprise of organized religion seriously or even morally compelling.

And so we have extremes, and with a shrinking moderate and faithful center. Membership in mainline Christianity in America is falling off the cliff, for both Protestant and Catholic communities. There seems to be no version of Christianity in America that is not experiencing a period of decline.[2]

Beginning in the 1960s, today we continue to depend on a broadcasting mode. Television, print media, internet . . . these have all been places where people are posting and pushing their versions of truth. But it isn't working. The extremists are broadcasting too. In a post-modern mindset and culture, moderates are not entirely sure what they believe about Jesus and so, at best, they broadcast welcome and inclusion but do not match the depth of their openness with deep teaching or deep practice. We moved from the burden of converting the world to broadcasting to the world.

The good news is that there is a discernable new movement of the Holy Spirit in our times. I believe we are being called to sharing our faith not as burden or broadcast but instead as blessing.

The Holy Spirit, who is both God and evangelist for God in the world, is at work everywhere to heal, liberate, and redeem. Every form of death died in the tomb, and resurrection is the first fact and act of the new heaven and the new earth. This is the message that God is spreading. Every one of us is invited to join God's mission. It is time to learn to bless the world with the gospel, not conquer it or rule it. The title of every person who says yes to this invitation to bless the world with love is evangelist.

1 ▪ *What Is an Evangelist?*

Let's take a minute to define and reclaim the term "evangelist" according to its ancient creation and context among the followers of Jesus. Scholars of the first and second century agree that the term "evangelist" was utterly unique to the followers of Jesus. The word *evangelium* in Greek and Latin is not found elsewhere in literature contemporaneous to the New Testament documents. Either the followers of Jesus coined the term on their own or it was created to describe the disciples by others. Either way, the word *evangelium* meant both "good news" and "messenger." Over time, we began to use the term "gospel" to refer to the "evangelium" or "the good news." It is unclear whether or not the "good news" was understood as the narrative of Jesus or as the person bringing the news of Jesus.

I love this historical linguistic ambiguity because it unveils a sacred truth about holy evangelism: what we say is only good news because of the way that news is actually transforming our lives. The evangelist that is being transformed by the love of God in Christ *is* the Good News in the flesh. A person being transformed by Jesus Christ through the Holy Spirit is the proof of the power of the gospel. A Christian is the gospel not because of what they say, but because of what God's love is doing to them and in them and through them in the world. You don't ever have to wake up in the morning and wonder how you can start being an evangelist each day. If you are following Jesus, your life is already an evangelist sharing the Good News of Christ with the world. Belief in Christ is not just an idea that you carry in your head. Living in a relationship with Christ is a real experience that is happening to your whole body and soul. The Good News is living in you and changing your life with love. Therefore, a disciple is an evangelist while she sleeps or while he sits in silence. A life being transformed by Christ is sharing the gospel with every breath. Your life has been part of God's evangelism of all creation since your baptism.

A Christian evangelist is simply a baptized person whose life inspires other people to become baptized people. The more aware you are of your identity as an evangelist by baptism, the more intentional you can be in how you share the gospel that is already transforming your life. Notice that I said, "whose life inspires other people," not "whose words inspire other people." The most powerful evangelism is the power of a life that is committed to the love and mission of Jesus Christ in the world. The person who has made this commitment and who has adopted spiritual practices to get better and more faithful in this commitment every day will inspire others to do the same. Words are important but they are not the only and not the most powerful way to share the love of God with other people. This is the crucial difference between the Christian evangelist and an evangelist for Facebook or Google. Brand evangelists have the challenge to convince people to become new customers or new consumers in a crowded marketplace. But Episcopalians believe that God is already present in every person's life. We are not sharing a new product. We believe that God knows and loves every person already and that the love of God is present in the lives of every person already. What is often missing in agnostics or unchurched people is the awareness, belief, desire, or ability of any person to hear the voice of God present and calling in their life.

Episcopalians believe that God is calling all people into deeper and deeper relationship, every minute of every day, whether a person

believes in God or not. Episcopalians believe that people are free to
ignore or reject the constant call of God in everyone's soul from
conception and through death. But we also believe that God will
not stop calling despite any person's inability or refusal to listen. In
our theology, humans are free to ignore God's voice, but our freedom
does not limit God's freedom to call and call and call again, in the
depths of every human heart and conscience. The Episcopal evangelist does not introduce God's love to a person, as if any soul had
never heard it or felt it. In the Episcopal tradition, we believe that
we are bringing Good News, not New News. We are not introducing
anyone to a new product or idea or service, like Lyft or Amazon or
Twitter. We are on God's mission to awaken every soul to the love
of God that is, from conception, at the core of their being and is
the source and end of all their longing and hope. In one of our
liturgical prayers for "deceased people who do not profess the Christian faith" in the *The Book of Occasional Services*, we pray:

> Almighty God, we entrust all who are dear to us to your
> never-failing care and love, for this life and the life to
> come, knowing that you are doing for them better things
> than we can desire or pray for . . . .[3]

God's love for every person is never-failing and God's love is present
in every person already. An evangelist listens to God to discern
how best to participate with God doing for others better things
than we can desire or pray for. In our prayers to bless evangelists,
we pray:

> Gracious Father, your Son before he ascended in glory
> declared that your people would receive power from the

Holy Spirit to bear witness to him to the end of the earth:
Be present with all who go forth in his Name. Let your
love shine through their witness, so that the blind may
see, the deaf hear, the lame walk, the dead be raised up,
and the poor have good news preached to them. . . .[4]

Notice the core convictions in this prayer. Preaching is only mentioned once in describing how an evangelist shares God's love with
the world. Before speaking at all, the prayer defines evangelism as
bearing God's love, healing illnesses, and even raising the dead.
The evangelist is a beacon of light and love, not a carnival barker
with a story to shout.

The evangelist uses his or her life to show people what listening
to God looks like. They clear the ears of the soul of others to hear
God calling within their own soul. We do this by listening to the
lives of others so closely, so compassionately, and so curiously that
we can find the voice of God calling in the lives of others.

Evangelists are seekers not salesmen. We do not bring God into
someone's life, rather we listen and study the joys and pains of
others—even in a first or brief encounter—to discern where God
is already calling and converting darkness into light.

You Can Be an Evangelist

Both extroverts and introverts can be patient and passionate listen-
ers for God, and the world needs both. Both personality types can
listen to the words and worries and wonders of another person
and help them hear the voice of God in all of it. Evangelism is
holy hearing and loving listening by any kind of person. We help
people hear God by listening to their words and stories, watching
their eyes and faces, and then pointing out where we see and hear

God's holiness, goodness, mercy, and love at work in their daily lives. In later chapters, we will consider precisely how to engage people about where God is in their lives.

In my experience, the most persuasive preaching is a life lived in faith. I can remember the names and faces of people in my life, all the way back to childhood, who were people of strong and contagious faith. Some of them talked to me about their faith or answered my questions about it. But others never mentioned their faith, or talked much at all. What drew me to them then and now was the observable transformation, love, and power of their lives. What made them my spiritual heroes was how their unique lives showed evidence of hope, faith, and love daily. My curiosity for their faith led me to ask questions, to pull words out of their lives. They were disciples of Jesus and it showed. And I knew miraculous transformation when I saw it.

Lives lived abundantly are evangelists more than any personality type. Jesus said so many life-changing things. But prophets before him had spoken powerful words about God too. Jesus lived his faith in a community that could watch him talk to God, take risks, experience suffering, heal the sick, expel demons, endure rejection, break bread, and love others heroically. Jesus was more than a preacher and teacher. His life was a walking explanation of and invitation to what it is like to know God and give your life over to God's presence and purposes. It is the life of Jesus that I have experienced in my baptism, in the Eucharist, and in my prayers and body that converted me to believing He is God. Though the scriptures have been indispensable in helping me recognize the presence of Jesus in my body and soul and in the world, there is no Bible verse attributed to Jesus that alone converted me to a belief that Jesus is God and that he can transform lives. It is the transformation I have seen in others who are following Jesus that has convinced me that following Jesus can transform my life too.

It is people that talk *to* God, not just *about* God, daily and authentically, that experience real transformation in their own lives. When their family, friends, and even strangers see that transformation, then others know something real is happening. It is that witness—the observable fact of something real that is happening in your life because of the love of God—that is the force that stirs others to ask you or others about your faith. Your words should not be necessary as commentary on something more real, more obvious, more unique, and more powerful than language can adequately capture. When people see you forgive the seemingly unforgiveable, give to the deserving, show mercy to the guilty, show love to the haters, show patience to the thoughtless, show kindness to the mean, show generosity to the selfish—then as Jesus said, "By this everyone will know that you are my disciples, if you have love for one another" (John 13:35).

If you don't know what to say about your faith or you don't know what words to use, there is a deep and divine truth in your hesitation. Words alone were never meant to be the witnesses of Christ to the world. It is you—your whole life, your body, your breath, your suffering, and your hope—that is the witness, the evidence, and the ultimate persuasion. Your life committed to Christ transfigures your humanity, not some turn of phrase. Do not traffic in terms, but delight in practicing the faith daily—seek the sacraments, read the Bible, say your daily prayers, love your neighbor—and the world will most certainly meet the Christ taking over your life. Believe that Jesus can live in you, and you in

Him, and before you ever open your mouth, Christ in you will be the light, the leaven, the salt, and the hope of glory that can convert the world to the love of God.

Remember we do not "do" evangelism for God. God evangelizes the world through those who choose to follow Jesus and to be filled with Christ in sacrament and prayer. Evangelists are the faucet of the living water with which God wants to bathe creation. You are the chalice, not the wine.

It is your life, not your words or lessons or sermons, that will turn other people toward God. If your life is being transformed in Christ, then others will see it, experience it, and seek it. God is contagious. Faithful followers get up in the morning and see their own lives as their mission field—they are the first convert from their choices each day. They spend their days drawing closer to God through prayer and fellowship and learning and liturgy and serving others. And, as their lives become more and more deeply rooted in the life of Christ—as their baptismal identity and its miraculous power becomes more and more the core and course of their life—other people around them will see God.

The 5 Steps of a Highly Effective Evangelist

1. Be a disciple.

2. Learn to recognize and follow the voice of God in your life through scripture, prayer, sacrament, and community.

3. Listen to other people share their lives with you, and listen for God's presence and voice in their story.

4. Name where you see God in their life story, using their words and their experiences.

5. Be ready to explain what you mean by God's voice and how you have learned to hear it. This last step is, for many people, the only step in evangelism. But although it comes last in joyful and liberating evangelism, it is nonetheless an important step.

2 ▪ *The Soul You Save Might Be Your Own*

A near-universal definition of evangelism is this: telling a story. Humans are storytelling people. If there is ever awkwardness with evangelism, let me suggest that it's a problem with the story, not the ability to tell it. The reality is that many Christians do not believe they have a powerful personal and transformational story to tell about knowing God.

Many of these people go to church. Some weekly and others only on holidays or for weddings and funerals. Many of them have been involved in leadership in their churches. They give time, money, and energy to their parish. In many cases, these churchy people were raised in homes where their parents or grandparents also attended a local church and gave a lot of their time and treasure to it. Statistics and demographics tell us that these multi-generational churchgoing families are more and more rare, though they were the backbone of local churches for hundreds of years in this country.

Membership in churches across mainline denominations is shrinking every year, and few churches are replacing the baby boomers as they age with younger families or young children. Yet there are many small churches across the country that open their doors on Sunday morning to some of the most hardworking and faithful followers of Jesus that American Christianity has ever seen.

Many churches are struggling to find new ways and new energy to find new members. We know church is important in knowing God, but to too many visitors to our communities, we look almost desperate. It is hard in any relationship to hide anxiety, frustration, or the shame of shrinking capacity. Elaborate and energetic welcoming ministries try hard to bring in new people and shower them with love and affirmation upon arrival and into the weeks after their first visit, but few churches have vibrant and sturdy ongoing fellowship and formation offerings for every age group.

We are thinking and talking and praying to keep our faith communities alive. It is no wonder that there is little space and oxygen left in any faith community or ministry for joyful or contagious conversations about how Jesus Christ is transforming our lives through the word of God and through the sacraments. Our communities face unprecedented challenges to sustainability and growth. It seems there is more of a call to rescue the institution than to rest in the presence of Christ at any moment. The institutional experience of church has become more important in our words and ways of being than the actual passionate and life-changing experience of following Jesus with others through every minute of every day.

Our theology proclaims that everyone is connected to God, but that truthful story and its liberation that lives deep within the human heart appears to have fallen asleep in many people and in many faith communities. We were created to live joyfully and eternally in the triune life of God, in Christ through the sacraments, and by the grace and ministry of the Holy Spirit on earth and beyond. We need to be more comfortable sharing the testimony of what it is like to be dead and risen in Christ.

How Do We Wake Up Our Stories?

For many people, the church building is their only personal or shared experience of God. The good news is that God does meet us in church buildings, and the people gathered are, in fact, the Body of Christ. To enter or abide in a church building of believers is a real experience of God. But for many, this communal experience of God rarely transforms their life and practices outside the building and its assemblies. Episcopalians are most likely to invite someone to visit their church than to sit in a home or the office or the field and pray or read scripture together.

The church buildings suggest and define the holy with Christian symbols, colorful windows of saints and biblical stories, and the architecture that reaches toward the sky. Our buildings are bursting with sacred stories, but are we?

Followers of Jesus are experiencing a living and eternal God in every breath they take. Any moment in human life can be a transformative experience of knowing God, and those stories are the most powerful stories any creature or creation can share. A thousand windows, a million altars, and a billion bricks of churches are a shred of straw compared to the presence of God through the Holy Spirit at the core of your being that is available and eager right now to hold you, to heal you, and to have you living in the perfect love of the Trinity forever. Right now.

What's It Like to Be a Christian?

When someone asks me what it's like to be a Christian, I do not start talking about what church I attend or churches I used to attend. Instead, I usually smile and thank them for asking me about the most important thing in my life. I start talking about what it is like to know and feel the creator inside my heart and to watch the transformation of every part of my life that I give over to that divine power within. I say how hard it is to hold to the belief with gladness and singleness of heart, but that in church and out of church, I find others who are also trying and praying, finding and trusting, naming and sharing their stories of knowing the same God in Christ.

We begin to awaken the story of us and God tucked within our hearts when we dare to go and dive into it, when we believe that when we seek the kingdom within our own soul, we find not just the image of God, but also the voice and the presence of God. *You* are a building with an altar in your soul where God meets you in prayer and praise and rest. Any building on earth is meant only to teach us how to find and mine the presence of God in the temple that we are. The building is for practice; it is not the precious pearl.

Generations of theologians have encouraged people with scripture and tradition that the church is not just a building, but also and more importantly the gathered people of God. Jesus taught that Judaism was more than the temple and that his followers were more than their upper rooms. This core message of the gospels is clear. Church is a people, not a place, and the church in your life is not the building down the street, but the place in your soul where you meet and know God.

Churches let people visit God. This is a gift. But the message that God is in churches is only the beginning of the Good News. If we are ever going to have a story of God and us that speaks to our whole lives, we must choose to enter a relationship with God that enters every minute of the seven days of the week. Christ offers himself to be the source, not a sporadic destination, of our joy. In Christ and through Christ, "we live and move and have our being" (Acts 17:28).

In a sacramental tradition, we certainly believe that material things matter and bring us into a relationship with God. We believe that candles and altars and fonts are portals to new life and sirens of eternal salvation. They both point us and draw us toward real moments with God.

But at a certain point, the idea of a church building as a destination to meet with God has become more important than its role as a threshold to eternal things. Remember the word *nave,* our word for the main space of the sanctuary. It is from the Latin word *navus,* meaning "ship." The purpose of the sanctuary space was to take you on a journey, not to be an end point of travel or a visit to a museum. The nave is not the destination. It is the ship to somewhere else, through song and scripture and sacrament. It is also a way to somewhere deep within yourself and to somewhere deep within the lives of those around you. The nave brings you to a new place of mystery and vocation, where you can dive deeper into yourself and dive deeper into the world.

Everything we see will pass away in the new heaven and the new earth and what will remain will be Christ in you, the hope of glory. That story, the story of Christ in you every minute of every day, challenging and changing you, helping and healing you, restoring and redeeming you, is the story of our souls living to tell the story our world is dying to hear.

Jesus and the Book of Common Prayer

We have not been formed to think of walking with Jesus with or without buildings every hour of every day in every place we breathe. If you read through the 1979 Book of Common Prayer, and certainly its predecessor of 1928, the name of "Jesus" as a stand-alone name is rarely used, if ever. More often we use the titles: Jesus Christ; Jesus, Son of man; Jesus, Son of God; Jesus of Nazareth. We are not, shall we say, on a first-name basis with Jesus in the Episcopal tradition. It is no wonder that talking then about "Jesus in your daily life" is not a way of talking or living that resonates with a lot of our people.

Prayer books by definition are not primarily descriptive manuals for being a disciple. They are, in the Episcopal Church, what we believe, but they often fail at describing how to come to believe. These lessons we need to write and speak and share with one another. Prayer books give us endless and beautiful words to say to God and about God and to express in our creeds and catechism what it is that we believe to be true. We have studied and taught much about our prayer books as holy transcripts to and about God. We now have to step up our game in teaching about how to see your life as a holy testimony of God's power and love, and how to show and share your life with Christ with others.

Going and Growing

When I ask many Episcopalians about God, they often start telling me about their church, what it's called, how old it is, how long that person has been a member. In fact, more than once as I've pressed people to tell me about God and less about their church, they have looked at me in the face and said that they don't know how to talk about God without talking about their church. We are shy about sharing our faith, because we are uncertain that our faith is making any daily or hourly difference in our lives. Being a member of a church is not the same thing as having a transformative relationship with Christ, though of course they can happen at the same time. When it comes to church, there is a difference between going and growing.

For centuries many have been going to church, but the question is, have they been growing in their personal and collective relationship with God? We have stories about going to church, but do we have stories about growing at church? I visited a church in Ohio recently and met a man named Bill. He walked up to me after I delivered a sermon and wanted to tell me about his faith. "I am 82 years old," he said proudly. He wanted me to know why he went to that church. "I learn something every week at this church, about God, and there aren't many places that think I still can." Bill doesn't just go to church. He is learning at church. He is growing at church. It is where he is learning to have an intimate relationship with God in his daily life.

This is why we speak of sharing the gospel in the world as reconciling the world with God. No one is introduced to God for the first time by another person. We are all created by and for God, but we also believe this freedom was given to all creation. To ignore the presence of God within us or name it or treat it as anything we want separates us from what God intended us to be.

I believe one reason we are not helping people find and know a personal relationship with God is that we talk less and less about the soul and instead more about the details of joining or maintaining a church. Read the prayers in the prayer book or the words of our hymns that speak endlessly about the soul of the person. In the Roman Catholic Church's Catechism, there is a definition of the soul that mirrors the Episcopal conviction that God is present and waiting to meet us in our soul at any time. This Catechism refers to the soul as one's conscience.

> For man has in his heart a law inscribed by God. His
> conscience is man's most secret core and his sanctuary.
> There he is alone with God, whose voice echoes in the
> depths.[5]

Episcopalians also believe that God's loving voice echoes in the
depths of all people, before any human person has ever spoken to
them, with or without any religious building or symbol. The evangelist is not bringing the voice of God to anyone, nor are we telling
people about a love of God that they have never known. We are
called to know and love people well enough to help them hear
that voice at the core and sanctuary of their own heart that has
been present since their creation. The evangelist is a kind of listening coach. Within every person is a story of faith—a story of a
loving God who speaks and listens, who hears and heals, who
forgives and loves us every second. This is the story we were created to share and that the world is dying to hear. This is the story
that the evangelist knows and shows to the world.

Searching for the Black Box

Think of the black box of an airplane. No matter how far beneath
the ocean, a crash can plant and hide that box in the deepest parts
of the earth. It is a great gift of technology that, in most cases, the
black box continues to send out a sound for those who are
listening.

How do we find the black box? Instruments of listening can
bring us closer and closer. When even the faintest ping is heard,
we know the direction to move to hear more. As one moves closer,
the pings gets louder, the sound becomes clearer, and we are able
to find and reunite with that which was hidden. As Episcopalians,

we believe this is the voice of God in a person. Because of all the freedom and suffering that defines human life, this voice of love is buried so deep, so far beneath the surface of daily life, that many people cannot hear it at all. It is our job as evangelists to dive into the oceans of other lives, to hear of their every current, of every still place, of every storm, of every crisis, and listen for what we trust as Episcopalians to be the presence of God in all of those experiences. Wherever their life has gone, God has been in them and with them and we are the listening instruments as evangelists who can find that ping, that presence of God in any human story, and help any soul hear the sound of God. We recognize the voice of the shepherd that we know through our own daily practices of reading scripture, of attending liturgies, of saying our own prayers, of asking God to make us better and better at hearing God's voice in all things, then we can point to God in the person's life.

It is not the ultimate job of the evangelist to point a person to a church or to point a person to an idea inside a person's head. It is instead to point the person to the voice of God in their daily life, to bring them into a listening relationship with that divine voice calling. That is the mission of an evangelist. We show and tell our stories as a way to familiarize people with what a story of God sounds like. Our story of what it is like to know, love, and be transformed by God is not a new story. We are not bringing the black box and planting the sound in a person's heart. Instead we are an instrument that lets the person find what has become hidden in their life. As Episcopalians, we trust that if we have done our job to help someone hear God in their life, we believe they and God will work it out. We have done the matchmaking, we have done the midwifing, we have been the microphone in the

17

depths of the ocean of the human condition that has done its best to make a holy voice louder. It is the voice of God we are trying to amplify in someone's life, not our own.

Do You Know What You Believe?

There has been much research on how little mainline Protestants, including Episcopalians, even know about their own faith. There is freedom that comes with admitting that we have an identity crisis and a lack of accessible and joyful personal stories of knowing God. We need a reset. We need to stop offering just social experiences at church. More and more, studies show us that people are only interested in church or religion because they want to know about God, not a book club, knitting group, or community service experience, although those can all be places to grow in your faith in Christ. Again, these experiences need to be the portals not the destinations of souls. How does knitting deepen your prayer life? How does the book you are reading help you discern God's challenges to your doubts or resentments?

In my teaching settings (seminaries, churches, schools, etc.), I often offer an open question and answer period at the beginning or the end of a class where people could ask anything they wanted about any part of Christianity. It is not that I think I can answer all of these questions, but I believe that we need to hear what people need to learn—and then as teachers of any value, we have to find a way to get them connected with that knowledge. Many times people who have worshiped in churches for decades ask the most fundamental questions about altars, the Bible, the saints, or the seasons. We need to be a faith community that builds the confidence of disciples with knowledge of our tradition as people who are in love with God and Christ and who know how to describe to other people how it is that they came to love God in Christ.

How do you fall in love? You long for it, or you meet a person that stirs longing in you. Either way, once it starts, you want to find out as much as you can about that person. This is why conversations can go on for hours at a time when a relationship first begins. If we want people in our faith communities to fall in love with God, how are we arriving in their lives as teachers and leaders to start meeting their longings to know God better, one question at a time. Liturgies help in that they expose people to the holy habits of disciples and to the sacred words of our tradition, but no one wants to know God in general. People want to know the things about God that emerge in their own hearts. Remember, God is speaking in their life, and there are times when the words of our liturgies or prayers do not reflect the conversation that God has been having with that particular person since their creation.

Are we asking people in our churches, "What do you want and need to know about God, to feel forgiven or more peaceful or more alive?" Our liturgies do stir our hearts and raise questions, but do we put as much effort into answering their longings that our holy liturgies awaken? Research shows that people choose churches because they want to know about God.[6]

What do we believe? I find a huge insecurity about our theological convictions. I believe this is at the core of why we do not share our faith convictions with others. People don't want to talk about their faith at work or at play if they don't know what to say. Without a personal relationship with Christ, you can't talk about it. If you don't understand much about the theological convictions of your community, then you're not going to say much about that either.

Many Episcopalians say they love the Episcopal Church because it doesn't "have any dogma." They have misinterpreted the openness and generosity of the Episcopal tradition to mean that there is no backbone and no absolutes. If we want people to share their faith in settings where people are talking or asking these kinds of questions, we must form folks with better answers. We want to be a safe place for all kinds of people, with all kinds or no beliefs. We are healthier for that openness. But we cannot let that openness decay the core convictions of our faith. A place to start is "An Outline of the Faith," commonly known as the Catechism in the Book of Common Prayer beginning on page 845. We are a people of deep, specific, and absolute claims. It is our commitment to deepen convictions that allows us to embrace the world so openly and so unconditionally.

Saint Paul warns against "zeal without knowledge" (Romans 10:1–3). This verse is less judgmental and more practical advice. Few Americans lack the zeal to share ideas, but if you do not have knowledge of the Christian faith, you will lack the confidence to show or share your faith.

Fly a Kite

For me, a powerful image of what an Episcopal evangelist looks like in the world is the image of a person flying a kite. We pick a kite that speaks to us: its color, its shape, its sturdiness. The kite is an expression of our passions and truths. You cannot fly a kite indoors; the success of flying it depends mostly on the wind over which you have no control. And so you set out into the world. The Holy Spirit is the wind that will or will not make the kite soar. The more a person knows about physics and kite flying, the better the experience will be. You can run to lift a kite even if there is very little wind. Skills matter. Knowledge matters. But in the end, the wind is stronger than any alternative. My great joy in kite-flying is to feel the strong tug on the string in strong wind as the kite dips and dives higher and higher. When the wind is strong, you don't even have to move your feet. The wind is the author of the outcome. I am in awe of the invisible and utterly unique power of something pulling the kite high into the sky, at times pulling so hard that the string might burn your fingers with its strength and the speed of the cord winging out of your hands.

I never tire of the holy experience: I show up with a kite that is a reflection of my loves, and when God shows up with wind, what I bring takes flight. The kite of an evangelist is their personal story of how God has changed their life. And it is God who will take that story and fly it high or low or at times, not at all. There are some things you can learn to work best with whatever wind there is. But the tug reminds you who is in charge. Sometimes we can join the evangelism that God is doing in a moment or in a life. The job of the Episcopal evangelist is simply to show up with the kite. It is God who puts the kite into flight.

3 ▪ *There Is No Public Square*

In ancient Greece, the *agora* was what we moderns would call "the public square." The literal meaning of *agora* is "gathering place." In city-states across the ancient world, the *agora* was the center of civic life at the heart of cities. Every public or town square since, in the western world, is a descendant of this idea of a central outdoor space of commerce and community. This is where workers and warriors, philosophers and politicians, shopkeepers and shoppers shared a common life.

Distinct but not disconnected from the *agora* were the temples and altars of a city to the Greek gods and goddesses (and later, after the conquest of Rome, to the Roman deities as well). The line was not so clear between religious space and civic space in Greco-Roman society. There were, in addition to large temples, small outdoor altars near those temples, in farmers' fields, near large homes, outside shops, or along city streets. The worship of gods—however automatic, cultural, unexamined, political, or shallow—could be seen in homes, streets, or farms, as well as in religious temples. These overtly holy places were mostly where people gathered for religious ritual, but they were by no means the only place to engage with or hear from the gods. The gods, in ancient understanding, had the run of the cityscape and the countryside, the temple and the town square, the hearth and the home. The membrane between any "public square" and the places of divine presence was profoundly porous. The holy ground and the playground of the gods was all earth. Temples and altars were not constructed to bring the gods into human space, but were built to bring humans into divine space, which could be anywhere.

The temples of emerging secular nation states—the churches and cathedrals of Europe and America—became the exclusive centers for worship and formation in religious identity and practice. This post-enlightenment retreat of religion from "public space"—making what is "public" something that is by definition secular—is a modernist experiment in which we still live.

What matters to me is the birth of the notion that the "public square" is somehow a formless void of God's real presence—a place religious people enter and bring with them their God. It is hard to find the moment or the century in which this became the norm in the imagination of monotheistic people. Prior to Constantine, Christians never knew public space as their own. The Coliseum with its public and playful executions of Christians and other religious minorities was the outrageous proof of who owned public space. But even in pre-Christian Rome, public space was still not secular space.

A wall of separation arose between church and state, even where the church was the state. There were places and spaces where religion had its place and had no place. Think of so many town squares in America today—many have a church at the center of things, often at an intersection of town halls, public schools, or commercial centers. And yet, the building itself is a sign that church is just one voice among many. And it's an inside voice, leading to the notion that one must walk outside the church to share and inside the church to care.

This idea—that there is objectively secular space and that religious individuals leave their churches, synagogues, or mosques in order to bring their holiness and their God into a spiritually empty or spiritually dead civic society—has been disastrous for religious people and for the world. Bad theology comes from such lies. And the lie that God dwells exclusively or even just more often in churches than in dog parks has led Christianity to both great courage and great crimes. When we accept the lie that there is such a thing as a "secular public square" in need of God's presence—a place on earth where God is not, unless we bring God in with us—we tragically burden ourselves to bring God where the Bible and sound Christian theology tell us God is already. We are called to go forth and baptize, not go forth and bring God to where God is not or not yet. Every form of imperialism, colonialism, patriarchy, slavery, crusade, subjugation, domination, and annihilation can root itself in this demonic idea that there are places without truth, grace, or God prior to someone bringing them. Evangelism that roots itself in the idea that one can or must bring God to somewhere God is not is heresy for anyone who confesses the Incarnation.

Today's Public Square: Expectation

Episcopalians are not pantheists who believe everywhere is God. We are Christians who believe God is everywhere. So free your evangelism from heresy. When you enter your church, sing "Emmanuel, God is with us." When you leave church to enter the world, sing "Emmanuel, God is with us." The unburdened evangelist knows God and walks to the ends of earth in communion with God, seeing the image of God in every new face and every new place and wanting to know God deeper in all of those moments of encounter. The evangelist recognizes God in themselves, and that recognition teaches them to find God in others and in other foreign places. The joyful and liberated evangelist expects to find God everywhere in creation, even in the darkest valleys of the shadow of death. Evangelism is not bringing God anywhere. It is expecting to meet God in all people and in all places and being ready to show and share this awareness with anyone you encounter, through listening and perhaps with words.

Evangelists have the gift of expectation. The evangelist is always looking for God, and this expectation of divine encounter anywhere and at any time in the otherwise secular culture challenges others to look as well. Have you ever had a meal with someone and you notice their eyes fixating on something besides you or their food, when their whole head turns and locks on something you cannot see? Every time this happens to me—whether I am the person who sees something new or I am the person who notices someone seeing something new—the same words immediately interrupt any conversation. Someone blurts out, *"What are you looking at?"* Our focused attention and contagious expectation to see God everywhere is perhaps our most powerful evangelistic skill. In contrast to (too many) trends in contemporary teaching on evangelism, the evangelist is not the person who is practiced in words. The evangelist is the person who is practiced in wonder. When we focus our gaze and ways on Christ, God often stirs the question in others, "What are you looking at?" or "Why are you living that way?" If someone asks you that question, you know you are practicing a fruitful form of evangelism.

Evangelism as Invitation

So why go anywhere and speak of God? If God doesn't need you to talk about God, then why bother? Even that question demonstrates a perception that God needs (or doesn't need) humans to do things. Think instead of invitation. When we look for a deeper relationship with God through praying more, reading scripture more, or attending the Eucharist more, God meets us. Through these pathways to grace we grow in faith and spiritual maturity. We change. And others around us change because of what is changing in us. Our transformation transforms the world. I visited a church in Pennsylvania that has a sign on its lawn: "Changed lives change the world." Indeed.

This is perhaps counter to what you have heard about evangelism. I find many books on evangelism do not trust in the persuasive power of transformation, focusing instead on how to bring God, with your words, into the secular public squares of your daily life. I am not saying that we do not need to speak any words about God to share our transformation. We are given language to proclaim what God is doing in our lives. St. Paul writes, "Always be ready to make your defense to anyone who demands from you an accounting for the hope that is in you" (1 Peter 3:15). But there is no point practicing your answer if you are not practicing the faith that brings transformation. Our words about why faith matters are aspirational if we are not practicing the faith, not experiential. And the people around us can tell the difference.

There is no public square where the Holy Spirit is not hovering over all as at the moment of creation. When you enter secular space, you are entering sacred space despite the power to profane that all humans possess and often parade. But God is already in every public space and busy. The evangelist shows up to take up a part of the ministry of love that God is doing everywhere and will continue to do on earth as it is in heaven. Evangelism is joining God's mission everywhere.

The Tower or the Shack?

A retired bishop of Sri Lanka was living in residence at the seminary where I live and teach. At that time, the guesthouse where he was staying shared a wall with our house. He was the most contagiously holy neighbor I have ever had. It was a glorious semester of learning from him and his wife about their fifty years of ministry in the church. He was about six-and-a-half-feet tall and always said the Eucharist gracefully, slowly, and in bare feet. His voice was deep and loving and wise. He loved to smile. He often spoke in parables and stories that I will never forget. He had been a priest and bishop in times of terrible war between the Tamil Tigers and the government. He knew murderers and he knew martyrs. Christianity is 7 percent of the population in Sri Lanka, so his faith was practiced and led on the margins of his culture. In retirement, he was preparing to serve the United Nations and work for human rights for the rest of his life.

While sitting on his porch one afternoon, we were deep in a conversation about the role of Christianity in countries where it is an extreme minority. I was also asking him what role Christianity can and should play in any country. I must have asked him a dozen anxious questions for every calm word he spoke. At one point, I think he decided to answer all of my questions with a single parable.

Looking out at the lawn he said, "Once upon a time there was a field on which someone wanted to build a tall tower. One day the builders set up a trailer on the site of the construction. And for weeks and weeks people came in and out of that shack to prepare for building the tower. Over time, blueprints were put on the walls of the shack and you could see its small lights glowing late into the night. Eventually, deliveries and cranes showed up and began to raise a building from the ground. Over time the tower got taller and the shack got older and more worn. Through the glowing windows of the shack at night, you could see birthday cards hung on the walls and leftover decorations from holidays; the grass around the shack was worn to packed dirt. One day, the tower was complete; within hours, the shack was put back on wheels and was gone. Only its imprint in the ground remained. By the next day, grass and flowers were planted and it was impossible to know the shack had ever been there." Then the bishop paused for a long time. Finally he looked at me and asked: "Which building is the church, the tower or the shack?"

The tower, said the wise man, is the kingdom of God, the new heaven and the new earth, the ultimate plan and promise of all creation. Bringing to life the plan—the dream for the tower—is why the shack was constructed. The dream was the permanent thing, the shack was the transient, though beautiful, reality. The kingdom of God is the dream of God for the whole world. And we, the church, are called to build that kingdom on earth along with God, in time and space. The church is simply the shack that comes into being for the purpose of building God's dreams for the world along with God. We are here to take a part in building the new heaven and the new earth. Christ died and resurrected for the world, not the shack.

We make shacks in the world to build community, to celebrate life, to mourn together, to sing together, to pray together, to share the sacraments together as we build the kingdom of God. Our vocations are not to build churches but to build the kingdom. In time, every single church on earth will pass away like a shack on a construction site. We ought to hold lightly the bricks and mortar of our buildings lest we fall into idolatry of them and think that their construction and maintenance is why we gather as a community.

We gather around the altar to go away from it, strengthened to build the kingdom of God that we experience at the altar. We are not here to stand at our altars any longer than is necessary to experience the kingdom of God. In time, every altar will vanish like a shack. But it is what happens at our altars, what the Holy Spirit does in us and through us, that will last forever. The sacraments build the kingdom of God in us and then we walk into the world and participate in building the kingdom of love and justice in the world. What is eternal is what we are building in our hearts and in the world, not the places where we gather to experience the grace of God.

What's Our Missiology?

The word "missiology" is just a fancy word for the study of the church's mission and purpose. Your missiology explains what you think the church is for, what you think the church needs to do, or what the church should not do. Almost everyone knows that the role of a "church" is to do more than simply offer a worship space indoors. If you think the role of the church is to teach people to make good moral choices, then that is your missiology. If you think the role of the church is to save people's souls from hell, then that's your missiology. If you think your church should be a physical sanctuary for political refugees in your city, then that is your missiology.

But does the Bible care which missiology you hold? Does Jesus? How do you form a missiology—a definition and direction for the church, the people of God on earth—that is true and liberating and holy? The truth is, different Christian denominations have different—deeply different—ideas about missiology. It was decades after I became a Christian that I started to think deeply and constantly about what my missiology is all about. I had spent years and years in church, praying for the world, coming in and going out in every worship service, but I had never thought seriously about why there is a church at all. Why is it that God creates us, enters into relationship with humanity, but leaves us here for a life on earth? Why are we not taken out of the world at baptism or when we choose to love God? Why this period on earth in which we wait for death followed by permanent and total communion with God forever? Why doesn't forever-with-God begin on earth and then take us out?

Let's begin with what we know: God created you and me and everyone for love, joy, and freedom. "For God so loved the world that he gave his only Son . . ." (John 3:16). A person's view of the church should begin with this vision; God does not need humanity to do anything in the world, but instead chooses to create us and invite us to share the world with God. At creation, God started the story of all things. At your birth, God started a unique story of your life. We were not created to work, even for good things. We were created for God to love us and invited to love God in return. And, to see others as also children of God, as our siblings in God, and therefore we love them and give our gifts and selves to them.

How do you know if your missiology—that is, your purpose, your mission for your gifts and time in the world—is true and holy? Here is a good rule: You should not hold a missiology, it should hold you. As Rowan Williams has written, "Christians do not have a mission, God has a mission and we are invited to join."[7] Your view of what the church's mission is should set you free, inspire you, bring you closer to God. This does not mean your definition of the church in the world should make you happy or comfortable. Jesus had a mission and it led him through Holy Week to a painful, lonely, and tortuous death. There was no safety; there was meaning and power and purpose.

That's what I want. I want meaning and power and purpose. And so my missiology is to listen for God, in every situation, and try to discern what God is doing and how I can join. If a person in the dog park starts talking and then starts crying through the story of their cancer diagnosis or their recent divorce, keep listening. Listen and ask questions about their feelings, about what surprised them in moments of grief or pain, where did light arrive, or what was the dark time like? Listen carefully and pray continually while you listen that God would show you where God is in the story. And then share it with the person. Naming God as a character in someone's story doesn't mean having to find something positive. Remember the suffering of Jesus. If a person's story seems drowned in pain and loneliness, perhaps Jesus was abiding in that pain with them and promising resurrection.

My missiology is based on the method of listening for God, praying continually to God for help in listening, and then focusing on finding and naming God in all things. My missiology is that there is no secular space that can banish the Holy Spirit. My mission is to find the Holy Spirit in the bank, the parking lot, the soccer game, or the hospital room. My purpose in life is to find the Spirit in my heart and in the world, living in that presence.

My missiology is to offer my life to the Body of Christ so that my ears, hands, and heart can be a symbol and a shepherd for others who are looking for the holy in themselves and in the world.

Your personal missiology should not be a personal project, made and managed by you alone. It should reflect what the scriptures say, what the sacraments are forming in you, what your prayer life is building in you, and what life in community with other disciples of Christ is teaching you. Our hearts join God's mission, they do not create one. I have found that the Episcopal Church's missiology sets my heart free. It holds me, guides me, challenges me, and draws me into community with other people. It is difficult to share your faith in the world when you are not sure why you should, or what happens to you or anyone else when you do. Taking time to consider and commit to a missiology can strengthen your resolve, your identity, and your energy for loving God and for sharing God's love.

Matthew 25 + Matthew 28 = Matthew 10

In my years as an evangelical in college with an organization called Campus Crusade for Christ, I remember hearing from leaders that there were two kinds of Christians. Even then I found it a narrow view of Christendom; the argument went something like this: "Matthew 25 Christians" are those that believe works of justice lead to salvation (". . . just as you did not do it to one of the least of these, you did not do it to me"). "Matthew 28 Christians" are those that believe preaching the gospel and leading others to accept Christ as Lord and Savior leads to salvation ("Go therefore and make disciples of all nations, baptizing them . . ."). In the Episcopal tradition, the truth is a mix and melding of the two. We all know people who have pitched their tent on one side or the other: the so-called Christian Right in this country who pray for the conversion of all people to the Lordship of Christ, and the progressive left Christians who march for causes and practice corporal acts of mercy with no overt mention of God in their work and no practice of the persuasion of others to a belief in God or Jesus Christ. Thankfully the Gospel of Matthew is only one of four rich gospels, and it also has thirty chapters to build a fuller picture of evangelism than two polar passages can provide.

I believe that the tenth chapter of the Gospel of Matthew comes closest to expressing an Episcopal understanding of evangelism. It goes without saying that Matthew 25 and Matthew 28 are essential passages to understanding and planning our lives as disciples of Jesus and members of his body in the Church. But if you asked me what kind of Christian I am, I would say that Episcopalians are "Matthew 10 Christians" because this chapter weaves together so many of the teachings of Jesus throughout the four gospels.

The tenth chapter of Matthew begins with ten crucial verses to describe the mission and the purpose of a disciple and of the church in the world:

> Then Jesus summoned his twelve disciples and gave them authority over unclean spirits, to cast them out, and to cure every disease and every sickness. . . . These twelve Jesus sent out with the following instructions: "Go nowhere among the Gentiles, and enter no town of the Samaritans, but go rather to the lost sheep of the house of Israel. As you go, proclaim the good news, 'The kingdom of heaven has come near.' Cure the sick, raise the dead, cleanse the lepers, cast out demons. You received

without payment; give without payment. Take no gold, or silver, or copper in your belts, no bag for your journey, or two tunics, or sandals, or a staff . . . . (Matthew 10:1–10)

These directions from Jesus to the twelve disciples are more overt than a parable and more comprehensive than a command to go forth and baptize. There are many things Jesus asks his followers to do. Notice how he tells them to start with people who are already (but fallen away) of the people of Israel. Jesus is sending his disciples to a place and people where God has already been present and potent. He tells them to remind the world that God is near to them and to speak of who God is. This is resonant with Matthew 28. And then Jesus calls them to perform immediate and transformative acts of liberation in people's lives. The sentences are short and direct: cure the sick, cleanse the lepers, cast out demons. Jesus is defining the disciple as one whose God changes things, real things, in real time. Curing, cleansing, and casting: these are all verbs that liberate those oppressed by illness and darkness of any kind. This is resonant with Matthew 25. Then the disciples are given the reason that they should give their lives away: you have received without payment, so shall you give.

Herein lies a powerful reason to speak about your faith in hopes to inspire others to find their own: we have received grace from God. Mirror that generosity. And lastly, pack light! The more we own, the more we are owned by the material world and its endless lust for more. This packing light means not only possessions but also perspectives. Enter the world as open as you can, do not bring many prejudices with you. This is today's public square.

4 ▪ *What Does Everyday Evangelism Look Like?*

I was heading off to the dog park after a long day at work and my dog had been trapped in the house all day. I was so eager to get to the park that I just threw the dog in the car and drove straight to the parking lot. When I got there, I realized I had forgotten a leash. The dog was so excited; he could see the park through the window and was jumping up and down, shaking the car on its wheels.

I looked everywhere. Did I have a belt? A piece of rope? Just anything I could use as a leash to get across the football field to the dog park on the other side. I then found a two-sided priest stole in my trunk. I had gotten the stole on Amazon for ten dollars, secondhand. It turned out to be a great leash.

I tied the end of it with tassels in gold around his collar and wrapped the other end, also with gold tassels, in my hand. I ran across the football field and walked into the park. Twelve different people asked me about this bizarre ornate stole. Not one of the twelve had any idea what it was called or exactly what it was for. About half of them had some sense that it was something you wear in church; all of them were curious why I had this shiny satin and holy looking fabric.

One person asked me, "Are you using that church fabric because it's Lent?" (It was Lent.) Then the man's wife turned to him and said, "What is Lent?" I mostly watched the couple teach other about what Lent is or might be, occasionally answering a technical question or just cheering on their shaky but important experiences and guesses about the season. One had "given up" things for Lent as a child. Standing there in the dog park, they both admitted that neither had gone to church for twenty years and neither had any idea what Lent, or for that matter, what Easter meant for their life in today's world.

Another person came up to me and said he had just done a DNA test on the dog that they rescued. He then, all of a sudden, looked at me in the face and said, "I haven't gone to church in twenty years." Something about holding the stole caused him to say something about church.

Someone else walked up to me and started conversations about the colors in the stole. She gave my dog some treats and then looked at me right in the face and said, "Do you believe in evolution or are you one of those Christians who doesn't?"

Another person came up to me and talked about how hard it is to cut the nails of his dog. The man then looked at me very quietly and said out of nowhere, "I don't go to church because I'm gay." He added, "But I miss going. A lot."

I never told anyone in the park I was a priest, but there was something about the symbols on the stole: the cross, some Latin inscription that no one knew. They all recognized my makeshift leash as somehow holy, allowing them to just start talking about religion.

I spent an hour in that dog park sitting on the bench talking with all different people, hearing about their experiences of Christianity, why they were in the church at one point then left, why they were curious about the church, or why they've never entered a Christian church since they were born. I heard about their suffering in life, their anger, their loneliness, and their joy. From the first conversation, I prayed constantly that God would give me ears to hear where God was moving in their lives. And I prayed for courage to say where I heard God in their stories. The stole turned out to be the spark—the conversation-starter. God opened the door in their hearts. All I had to do was listen and look for God in their words.

Never Too Late

One weekday, I was scheduled to celebrate the Eucharist at a church right across the street from the White House, St. John's Lafayette Square. There is a service there every day at 12:10 p.m. It usually ends at 12:30 or 12:35. It is a short service of prayer and sacrament, but a gift to the neighborhood of workers and tourists.

On that day the congregation was a very small but faithful group of people and it was glorious. I literally bounced around the aisles, teaching about and encouraging everyone to take in the liturgical season we were in, which at that point was Pentecost.

After the liturgy was finished, I walked outside the church to chat with the small group from inside and to shake their hands or high-five people at the curb as they headed back to their offices and daily lives. As I turned to go back inside the church, a young adult African American woman jogged up to me from the street and gasped, "Did I miss it?" She had, in fact, missed it. It was almost 12:45 but I smiled and said to her, "You did miss the 12:10 Eucharist, but if you have a few minutes, we could go do it again." She sighed with relief.

As we walked inside and down the aisle toward the altar, she noticed we were alone. "Is it just us?" she said sheepishly. I pointed to the colorful church windows and said, "You and me and every saint ever."

I invited her up to stand at the altar and said we would "share the altar book to read our parts." She paused at the altar and said, "I can't go up there. I'm a Baptist." I smiled and said, "So was St. John." She laughed, and then I heard her whisper as we approached the altar, "If Granny could only see me now."

What unfolded was a joyful instructed Eucharist, where I both said the words and then looked at her and explained why I was saying them, and invited her to say every word in the altar book that was not essential to be said by a priest. As you can imagine, she did most of the talking. We even briefly talked together about the reading of the day before we began the Eucharistic prayer. I told her that our conversation would be the sermon.

She had so many questions about God and every part of the Eucharist. She kept apologizing for asking questions while we were saying the prayers. Once we finished, she asked if she could stay alone in the church and pray. I pointed to every pew in the room and told her to pick one, and I left her and walked back toward the church door.

When I looked back over at her, she was quietly singing and tearfully praying. Eventually, she stood up and came to where I was at the door and as she left she said, "I am so blessed right now. I was walking to Starbucks for lunch, but I passed this church and felt God calling me in. I haven't been right with God for many years, but I just got right."

She was looking for God. It was my job to come alongside her and find a way to keep looking for God together. Her curiosity changed the words of the prayers for me too. Her curiosity fired mine, and words and images that had become commonplace seemed to jump off the page with power and promise as I read with her. I could hear in her voice, I could see in her face, that she had hit a moment of unbelievable and unmanageable longing for God and it was contagious. I could feel in her presence when she ran up to me that she was following God somewhere. All I knew for sure was that I wanted her to keep going.

It was not my job to take her hand and lead her anywhere. It was my job to get out of the way, to come up next to her and say, "Let's keep going. Whatever brought you to this curb and up to me in these vestments, let's keep going. You're looking for God, and I think I know where you can find more of the God who's speaking to you right now."

Grace in the Golf Cart

God moved a maintenance man in an RV park saying, "I am an agnostic Trump guy" to "Well, I hate the hypocritical church but I do miss God. I wish I could start over with him."

It turns out this was a man who was beaten by nuns in childhood while his best friend was raped by their priest. "I hate the church," he said. How did I respond as he seemed to pour his heart out outside the park's bathroom? I said, "I hear you. That was evil. I believe it makes Jesus weep. I believe he's still weeping."

We'd already gotten into talking about his faith. My spouse and I made him some Cuban coffee out of our RV and then added some honey to it. Finally, he asked if I needed any help. I shared I was about to walk to the RV shop to get some needed wood. He offered to give me a ride in his golf cart; we got in and took off. Little did we know that his reconciliation with God was underway.

On our golf cart ride, we laughed about our lives and shared prayers we had said as children in the Catholic Church. He said he missed God; I said he could start over with God. He said he did want to start over with Jesus; I said that he could at that moment in the golf cart. "Is it that easy to start over with God?" he said. I answered, "It's not easy. It takes everything you have and everything you are, but it is real because God is real. When you start over with God in Christ, you will find freedom you have never known. You don't have to figure out how to start over. The Holy Spirit takes over when you ask."

I learned he was a grandfather who loves children's books. I mentioned how *The Velveteen Rabbit* became real. The man smiled an excited smile. "How does this actually work?" He had previously mentioned that he used to work as an electrician. "Well," I said, "think of yourself as the plug and God is the outlet. Love is the power that comes into you when you plug in. Sit still with me now and let's feel it. Jesus has been close to you all the time that you have felt like you were walking away." I told him you can't leave Jesus behind because Jesus is within us. Jesus does not obey buildings nor does he condone the evil that might happen in them. God is always nearer than we think or feel.

He sat quietly. He then said, "I haven't been to church in forever." I responded, "The Bible says that where two or three are gathered with God, that is the church. This RV park is the church. My wife and I, if you join us, we will be two or three together, so welcome back to church." The small talk of hearing about his grandchildren and children's books, being an electrician, and his suffering allowed me to connect the gospel to his passions and pain. Listening to him was the way to speak to him about God.

Theology and Dermatology

Sometimes evangelism is just seeing God in someone else and being blessed by the vision. Sometimes these experiences for me are not from anything I say or do, but rather someone makes *me* feel closer to the God that is in my life. I experienced God deepening my faith through my new 75-year-old Jewish dermatologist.

Sitting in the examining room waiting, he entered and introduced himself to me for our appointment. Noticing the priest's collar I was wearing he said, "I am Jewish, I am an atheist." I smiled and said back, "I am Irish, I am a theist." He laughed.

After my exam, he confessed, "My parents were prisoners in the Dachau concentration camp. They survived but I cannot believe in God." My response: "What were their names?" He then pulled out his iPhone and started to show me pictures of his parents and the many relatives who did not survive the Nazis. I was surprised how quickly he was able to access these photos on his phone and it was clear that although these people lost their lives decades and decades ago, he somehow must look at these pictures fairly often or maybe show them to other people regularly.

I learned that on weekends he attends World War II re-enactments. He showed me pictures of himself in an Allied Army uniform along with other dressed-up friends that share the same hobby. "It's communal and fun," he said, but then added, "but inside, it also feels like fighting back."

I asked if he knew Hebrew. "Yes." I asked him if he knew Yiddish. "Of course." I asked if we could sing any favorite song of his from the Seder because I would love to sing with him. He was stunned. "Really?" he said. "Yes," I answered. "Pick one or I will!" He pulled up the lyrics on his phone of *Dayenu,* a very common song from the Jewish Seder. We sat together, sitting on the exam table singing *Dayenu* in Hebrew and we laughed. I hugged him at the end of our singing and said, "Your life is a miracle and you have blessed me." On my shoulder, before we let go, he whispered, "Maybe I am not an atheist. I am just very mad at God." When I pulled away and looked at him, I smiled. I took his face in my hands, holding his cheeks, and said, "C. S. Lewis used to call himself an atheist and he once wrote:

> I was at this time living, like so many Atheists or Antithe-ists, in a whirl of contradictions. I maintained that God did not exist. I was also very angry with God for not existing. I was equally angry with Him for creating a world."[8]

"You see?" I said to him, "You are not alone in that feeling of being so angry at God. It feels like unbelief. Many people do not believe in God because they are too mad at God for the way things have gone in life. That anger is also passion. Being mad at someone for not showing up when you need them is not the same as not believing in them. In fact, it's believing in them so much that you feel betrayed by something that appears to you as their lack of love." I smiled at him and said, "I see in you passion for God, not aversion." The doctor laughed at me and said, "I like you. And I like that guy C. S. Lewis."

I told him that I too thought God was angry about the Holocaust, and he simply nodded. He then started quietly to cry. I did as well and as we walked out of the exam room and down the hall, he opened the door for me to leave his office and said, "Shalom."

5 ▪ *Joining Joy*

Here are ten specific practices for strengthening your liberating and life-giving evangelism skills.

Greet God

It is a practice in the Anglican/Episcopal tradition to begin every day with the realization that God is already waiting for your awareness. God has been with you as you sleep. God is with you as you wake, and God's work has been at work in the world while you slept. It is important to keep this in mind because it can release you from the burden that you must wake up and begin God's work in the world anew. Waking up to an awareness that God is near to you and is at work around you already is a blessing. Do not begin the day wondering what you will start doing with or for God. Begin the day by greeting God who is already at work in you and giving thanks.

Pray Without Ceasing

Once you first become aware of God's presence and loving action in your day, begin to ask God how it is that you should respond and perhaps participate in what God is doing. Start a conversation, silently or aloud. If you do not know what to say to God, then say that you don't know what to say. Ask the Holy Spirit to speak through you, as St. Paul describes in his letter to the Romans.[9] Notice the first thing that comes to your mind, whether it is an anxious thought, a grateful feeling, or a confused mood. It is the Holy Spirit that talks to God. We are given the gift to have the Spirit pray to God through us. Simply ask to join in the communion of the Trinity that prays eternally in perfect love. It is truly amazing grace that we can enter this eternal and dynamic prayer. As we join in together in prayer, the Triune God enters our life. You do not have to *do* the work of prayer. But you do have to ask God to enter your life through prayer. Praying is not just kneeling or folding your hands, though both can help you focus on the presence of God in your heart. Prayer is also listening, wherever you are, to what God is inviting you to share.

Stay in Your Lane

As you get into conversations with people about God, whether they are close friends and family or someone you are meeting for the first time, you may be asked about things you know nothing about. Remember that God has called you to listen to others and help them hear God, not to be a teacher or expert on faith. Quite often, someone who cares a lot about such things as nanotechnology, international law, or theoretical physics starts a debate with us about why it is that God cannot be real from their perspective. At those moments, we have to remember to stay in our lane and stick to the Good News that is in our life.

Remember, God is in your life. These are the moments when, say, there are things you do not know and do not understand, maybe even things about which you're not even curious. Share the story of what is happening in your life. Name what you hear as holy in the life of the other person. Despite all the argumentation from someone who is an expert in things you are not who is standing across from you, you are an expert in the way God is transforming *your* life. Keep your words in that place. If you're a teacher, explain how God has changed your life of teaching. If you are an artist, explain how the grace of God is allowing you to create things far beyond your own imagination. Stay in your lane. Ask about their curiosity and what knowledge they don't have but long to have. Find communion in curiosity.

Play a Home Game

Whenever you're engaging in conversation with other people about their beliefs or yours, it can be easy to fall into areas that they care deeply about and you don't. That is like playing an away game—you are somewhere doing something you know how to do, but you're doing it in a place that is unfamiliar to you, surrounded by people who are unfamiliar to you. Having a "home court advantage" in athletics is how people tend to do things better when they are in a familiar place. By playing a home game, speak on experiences you have had personally or read about personally. Only talk about topics for which you have passion and a story. Avoid the shallowness of speaking that is all too common in our culture. Offer the person your deepest convictions, humor, and honesty. Speak your truths in love.

You also do not want to manipulate a conversation; don't change the subject to places that they do not want to go. Realize that the person will be more apt to be honest and curious if your conversation feels like a home game for them too. This means you cannot show contempt or be condescending. If they are an expert in something, ask them about it and show respect for what is honorable in their life. At all times, ask God to help you through each sentence of a conversation, keeping it where you feel comfortable and where you're making claims about things that are actually happening in your own life. Stick to the truths of the transformation of knowing God, and trust that the person to whom you are speaking is already having a daily experience of God at all times. Can you help them see where God is moving and speaking to them?

Let the Person Talk

All learning theory points to the reality that when people have an opportunity to speak or think during a lesson or a lecture from another person, they will gain more information. Giving people the space to express themselves gives them an opportunity to grow and challenge themselves to try on new ideas and thoughts. If your voice runs or rules the conversation, the person may stop listening, much less grow as a result of what you're saying. Don't just ask questions and then respond. Ask questions and then, ask more questions. A helpful phrase to keep the conversation open to the other person is to say repeatedly, "Say more." I have found that it is a blessing and encouragement to people when they finish a sentence or story and hear you respond, "Tell me more about that." In a culture of rushing, distractions, and multi-tasking, it can be such a rich blessing and sign of holiness to show someone you are ready and curious to hear as much as they want to share. Sometimes showing such generosity and patience is, itself, showing someone the unconditional love of God. Sometimes the best evangelism is simply generous listening.

Keep It About Jesus

The desire to know God is the deepest longing of any human person. God has given us the opportunity to show and share with others, both in love and in language, who God is to us. At the end of the day, the person with whom you're speaking may never talk to you again. If you stick only to the details of your own life, not keeping Jesus and what he's doing in your relationship together at the center of the conversation, it's possible that the person might, in fact, be learning only about you and not how God is transforming you. That night when they go to sleep, who would you like them to remember? You or the one who is changing your life?

Don't Keep It Simple, Keep It Sacramental

The goal of the Episcopal evangelist is not just to tell people about God, but to share the unique, beautiful, and transformative experience of knowing God through the Word made flesh in scripture and sacrament. Do not dumb down your conversation with discussing a generic Christianity. When you are speaking to an atheist, you might have to keep the conversation on the basic question of whether or not there is a God. But keep focused on the longing that you hear in the person while you pray (simultaneously in your mind) during the conversation. When you speak about your experience of God, do not try to keep it simple. We do not have a simple longing for God in our hearts, nor do we have a simple relationship with God. The longing for God in the human heart is deep, wide, and complex. It is the deepest and the widest longing that we have. Respond to and respect that longing with a testimony of your own life that is as complicated as you are. Don't just say you "go to church." Why do you go? Do you like the smell of incense? Do you feel whole by praying particular sentences in the liturgy? Does gathering with other disciples inspire you to do something specific? It was C.S. Lewis who once said:

> It is no good asking for a simple religion. After all, real things are not simple. They look simple, but they are not. . . . Besides being complicated, reality, in my

experience, is usually odd. It is not neat, not obvious, not what you expect. . . . Reality, in fact, is usually something you could not have guessed. That is one of the reasons I believe Christianity. It is a religion you could not have guessed. If it offered us just the kind of universe we had always expected, I should feel we were making it up. But, in fact, it is not the sort of thing anyone would have made up. It has just that queer twist about it that real things have. So let us leave behind all these boys' philosophies— these over-simple answers. The problem is not simple and the answer is not going to be simpler either.[10]

Talk About Freedom

Whether someone believes in God or not, in my experience there is one word that describes a great deal of the longing of all people, religious or not: freedom. The most frustrated people I see are those whose freedom has been in some way cut off, strangled, or threatened by someone or something in their life. The saddest people are those who have had part of their freedom, whether it's health, financial stability, or a relationship, taken away. They do not feel capable to love, heal, play, or move on. It is human to long for freedom.

One of the great gifts of salvation is freedom from death. This is the core of Christian longing and promise. Christ has defeated death, the great darkness and the longest shadow in human experience. The Good News is that no matter who you are, death cannot destroy you or keep you from the eternal love God has for you. Disciples are free from death in all its forms of decay, divorce, and discord.

According to our deepest Christian convictions, in rising from the dead Jesus has freed us from the power of death. We are not free from the experience of death, but we are free from its sting, from its power to take away our freedom to love and be loved. The freedom in Christ is eternal, and it is transformational for our ability to enjoy other things and other people, to endure the pain and the struggle in life, and to embrace the inspiration that we get from all things beautiful. In my experience of talking to people about God, I notice again and again how challenged and inspired people are when I keep my focus in our conversation on how faith has freed me from fear and from all forms of death.

Diversity Matters

Since we believe that Christ is at work in all people, it is important in our listening and our speaking to demonstrate openness to the fact that God is present in all kinds of people. We cannot underestimate the danger and the damage of speaking to someone as if we have in mind a kind of person that God longs to know and to love, or a kind of life that God prefers beyond the moral life.

In your conversations and listening with other people, speak and ask questions about the diversity of their life. Name and celebrate the differences between that person and you, between that person and other people. Let them feel seen in all that they are; every person with whom you are speaking about God is an image of God. Look into their eyes, enjoy their face, be curious about their expressions, movements, and mannerisms. You are in the presence of an image of God; that reverence, awe, and wonder can change the person's life to whom you are speaking. Tell the person if something they say or do reflects God.

Do not be shy about the wonder and awe that you feel when you realize that the person with whom you are speaking is bringing a version of Christ into the world that has never been, and that will never be again. Tell them that.

Talk to People with God

We are not mercenaries, who for our own salvation serve the pleasure of God or the purpose of God. We are members of the Triune life of God through Christ with the Holy Spirit in our lives. As we enter conversations with other people, remember that you are not talking about God as if God is some loving person back in your apartment or dorm room, or someone that you might meet if you walk a little further in the dog park. In all the conversations we have with people, we are also joined by God who is already at work in the lives of others. It might be a good idea when you're having a conversation with someone to picture an empty seat, a chair next to you and the other person, representing God present in the conversation, giving you words, extending your attention span, bringing you peace, patience, and a sense of holy curiosity. God is present to help us find the voice and presence of God in others' lives.

6 ▪ *The Myths Might Be Right*

Anyone who wants to share a story of any kind with other people should not ignore the widely popular and compelling stories in our culture being written and told. Evangelists do well to study great stories and why people love them. When a story is captivating or contagious in a culture, we learn something about the longings and the imagination of people who are touched, inspired, or even enraged by it. A great epic that is cherished and passed on from generation to generation tells us a lot about what people value, hate, fear, love, and what they might be willing to sacrifice. Some larger-than-life stories are known throughout a nation, like the ride of Paul Revere. Other stories are shared through a religion, like the narratives of the life of the Buddha. And yet there are also epic stories that exist only through intergenerational family storytelling. I am sure your extended family passes on and cherishes generations of stories about immigration, love, sacrifice, illness, miracles, or tragedy.

Evidence that there is immutable and eternal truth in human experience—truth deeper than any one context, culture, or any particular collection of convictions in any one time in human history—is found in the clear similarities and patterns among powerful myths from across the world. Thinkers like Carl Jung and Joseph Campbell spent decades of their lives studying the patterns in the epic stories in Western civilization. C.S. Lewis, J.R.R. Tolkien, and other great storytellers and story scholars in the twentieth century argued the patterns of epic stories are a result of the real presence of eternal truths in human experience. They believed God designed into the world natural, moral, and spiritual laws that govern all human experience. Universal truths do not dictate, but nonetheless steer the stories we tell. If the sun rises in the sky every day, whether anyone believes or denies it, we should expect that stories about its rising will pervade the stories of all cultures across time. The truth of the rising sun can be described in infinite ways that reflect the vast diversity of human storytellers. But no story in the world can stop the sun rising tomorrow. Some things are just true.

If you believe in a loving God who created all things and who wants to know and love all creatures in a relationship rooted in their freedom and willingness to participate, then we should expect that all of human existence will be full of sign posts, clues, and magnets toward the truth of God's existence and love. Episcopalians believe that creation is embedded with clues and keys to seek and embrace God's love. We are free to follow these natural and spiritual trails to their Creator, but we are not free to live in a world without them. A loving God would not coerce any creature into a relationship, nor should we expect that a loving God will leave creatures without maps of truth toward love, freedom, forgiveness, redemption, and joy. In Christian theology, the world is a landscape invaded by God's love constantly and compassionately. The Incarnation itself is the greatest example of a God who enters creation as a human life, to ensure that any person might find the way into the very life of God by the gift of a human guide.

We believe that the whole earth, and therefore every human heart, experiences the presence of God's love along with the Incarnation and the resurrection every second. We should therefore assume that no matter what a person believes or not, they live in a world and in a body with an ever-present loving God and an ever-present invasion of resurrection with its liberating joy in human experience. God is telling every heart, every second, what is true. These truths are like the rising sun. All humans are free to write or embrace any story they like, for or against these truths. Over each storyteller and story-listener, the sun rises every day. The most compelling stories weave into their narratives truth that is recognized by all humanity, whispering things that they already know, though only in parts. The epic story of a loving Creator echoes in the depths of every human heart. Any story written or told by humans that contains elements or patterns of that ultimate sacred story at the core of all us will awaken a person's deepest longing. Epic narratives are mirrors that show us the grand story of God with us that we all carry.

C. S. Lewis and his drinking friends (who called their clique "The Inklings") believed strongly that cherished myths of any culture are only treasured because they are connected to the story of God, the Incarnation, and resurrection. The power of particular stories is not their own. Not all tales contain the elements or patterns of the Christian story, but the ones that do The Inklings called True Myths. True Myths are stories from any culture that resonate with the Christian story of creation and redemption, reflecting its arc and ending.[11]

Let's consider three of our culture's most popular epic narratives in the last fifty years. They share elements and patterns that reflect the Christian story which helps to explain their vast reach and transformative power. They are True Myths. They whisper truths to the human spirit in a language the soul already knows. They depict passionate adventures undertaken with others toward love and redemption, for which humans long for at their core.

All three of these stories are often called a Hero's Journey, a term coined by Joseph Campbell to explain the architecture of powerful myths. But stories that are deeply connected to the Christian gospel are more than the story of a single hero with sidekicks or loyal friends. A story whose power is linked to or derived from the narrative of Jesus Christ might more accurately be described as a "heroic community journey," reflecting the desire and design of Christ to gather disciples into a Body that would be the Church until the end of time. *Star Wars, The Lord of the Rings,* and *Harry Potter* all have strong individual heroes; anyone who has read a chapter of these epics knows that the fellowships between friend and kin in these stories explain any success, victory, or redemption of the lead heroes.

I suggest meditating on these contemporary epic myths. They are now more widely known and spread than any monotheistic religion in America. They all derive their power from the true story of a Triune God who loves and redeems the world. Each shows us the power of the gospel story, even in forms that are just an echo of it.

In comparison, the institutional church has suffered a failure of the imagination. We have lost the vision or perhaps the ability to share the gospel as the epic story that it is—a story that already rests and speaks at the core of all human souls. God's love for us is the most epic story; it already sounds and sings within human souls.

To reinvigorate our evangelism, we need to recover and revive the joy, exhilaration, suspense, hope, heroism, high stakes, drama, and destiny of the gospel. These three epics have inspired hundreds of millions of people. Perhaps studying them will help us reconnect with the epic gospel that gave them birth.

Learning Evangelism from Jedis, Hobbits, and Wizards

It would be hard to find people in the English-speaking world that have not heard of *Star Wars, The Lord of the Rings,* and *Harry Potter.* When you consider these three epic stories side-by-side, four distinct themes emerge that help to explain why hundreds of millions of people continue to be inspired by virtues such as love, hope, forgiveness, community, sacrifice, and redemption. Let's learn from the stories that are transforming those around us. If it is true that many epic stories have as their DNA pieces of the love and power of the gospel, then as we delve into these narratives we too will hear whispers of the Good News that lives in our hearts and we will be blessed by the Word within us.

Four Elements of an Epic:
Call, Mission, Community, Destiny

Each of these stories begins with a trusted mentor who issues a clear and urgent call to a younger and often uncertain person. Had the mentor not found the moment and the words to issue a clear invitation to accept a call, the younger person might have wandered away from their vocation. In the opening chapters of the Harry Potter story, the gentle giant Rubeus Hagrid announces to Harry Potter his identity and call.

> Hagrid: You're a wizard, Harry.
>
> Harry: I—I'm a what?
>
> Hagrid: A wizard. And a thumping good one at that, I'd wager. Once you train up a little.
>
> Harry: No, you've made a mistake. I can't be . . . a—a wizard. I mean, I'm just . . . Harry. Just Harry.

Hagrid: Well, Just Harry, did you ever make anything
  happen? Anything you couldn't explain when you
  were angry or scared? . . . Ah![12]

This conversation is similar to the opening scenes of the first Star
Wars film (*A New Hope*) when the old hermit Obi-Wan Kenobi
announces to young Luke Skywalker that Luke needs to respond
to the obvious evil and corruption of the galaxy, choose a new
path for his passions, and learn new things because the universe
needs his help.

Obi-Wan: You must learn the ways of the Force if you're
  to come with me to Alderaan.
Luke: Alderaan? I'm not going to Alderaan. I've got to
  go home. It's late, I'm in for it as it is.
Obi-Wan: I need your help, Luke. *She* needs your help.
  I'm getting too old for this sort of thing.
Luke: Listen, I can't get involved! I've got work to do!
  It's not that I like the Empire, I hate it, but there's
  nothing I can do about it right now. It's such a long
  way from here.[13]

Though Luke at first rejects this call, the death of his family leads
him to return to Obi-Wan and say, "I want to come with you to
Alderaan. There's nothing for me here now. I want to learn the
ways of the Force and become a Jedi like my father."[14]

In *The Fellowship of the Ring,* the young Hobbit Frodo learns
that he has been given a ring from his uncle. He did not choose
it. And over time, Frodo learns that the ring must be destroyed
by someone pure enough to carry it, but not be corrupted by it.

Frodo is not forced to accept this challenge. But when he hears of the peril facing Middle Earth, he decides to answer the call to destroy the ring that chose him. "I will take it," Frodo declares, "I will take the Ring, though I do not know the way."[15] Like Luke and Harry, Frodo ultimately accepts his call, knowing that there are many things he will need to learn from others. More than Harry or Luke, Frodo often doubts his call after he accepts it, but is periodically reassured by mentors like Gandalf and Galadriel. In fact, Galadriel speaks these shepherding words to Frodo, acknowledging both Frodo's frailties and his calling: "Even the smallest person can change the course of the future."[16] Elrod the Elf makes a similar point:

> The road must be trod. But it will be very hard. And neither strength or wisdom will carry us far upon it. This quest may be attempted by the weak with as much hope as the strong. Yet such is oft the course of deeds that move the wheels of the world: small hands do them because they must, while the eyes of the great are elsewhere.[17]

At moments of doubt and loss, all three epic heroes are inspired by the urgency and inspiration of the mission. When it is clear that Voldemort has returned and is gathering followers, listen to what Harry Potter says to his friends:

> Harry: I've been thinking about something Dumbledore said to me. Hermione: What's that?
> Harry: That even though we got a fight ahead of us, we've got one thing that Voldemort doesn't have.

Ron: Yeah?

Harry: Something worth fighting for.[18]

At a time when Frodo is nearly ready to die from the struggles of his mission, the simple but utterly devoted Hobbit Sam Gamgee shares these beautiful and uplifting words with Frodo:

> It's like in the great stories, Mr. Frodo. The ones that really mattered. Full of darkness and danger they were. And sometimes you didn't want to know the end. Because how could the end be happy? How could the world go back to the way it was when so much bad had happened? But in the end, it's only a passing thing, this shadow. Even darkness must pass. A new day will come. And when the sun shines it will shine out the clearer. Those were the stories that stayed with you. That meant something, even if you were too small to understand why. But I think, Mr. Frodo, I do understand. I know now. Folk in those stories had lots of chances of turning back, only they didn't. They kept going, because they were holding on to something. That there is some good in this world, and it's worth fighting for.[19]

None of the heroes are told by their mentors or friends that they will be safe or even that they will live through the journey. The comfort comes in knowing that the mission is larger than any one person and has an impact on the whole world. Aragorn shares this powerful exchange with the young warrior maiden Eowyn, just before she dies in battle:

"The counsel of Gandalf was not founded on foreknowledge of safety, for himself or for others," said Aragorn. "There are some things that it is better to begin than to refuse, even though the end may be dark."

"What do you fear, lady?" he asked. "A cage," she said, "To stay behind bars, until use and old age accept them, and all chance of doing great deeds is gone beyond recall or desire."[20]

Eowyn would rather die serving a larger cause than live doing no "great deed." She agrees with Sam Gamgee that "there's some good left in the world, Frodo. And it's worth fighting for."

Just as the Jedis teach one another, Harry trains with his friends in the Room of Requirement for months in order to fight Voldemort and all the corruption of the magical world. Harry inspires his friends while they train in secret, reminding them that together they can learn skills that would be impossible to figure out on their own. Harry calls out during a lesson in which students are teaching each other, "Every great wizard in history has started out as nothing more than what we are now: students. If they can do it, why not us?"[21] Whether it's hobbits or wizards, these epics prove that the skills needed to fight evil are learned in community and tested by individuals who are surrounded by fellowships of friends. When Harry decides to leave Hogwarts for a fight with death eaters in London, he tells his friends that he must go alone. But Neville Longbottom protests:

"We were all in Dumbledore's Army together," said Neville quietly. "It was all supposed to be about fighting You-Know-Who, wasn't it? And this is the first chance we've had to do something real—or was that all just a game or something?'

"No—of course it wasn't," said Harry impatiently.

"Then we should come too," said Neville simply. "We want to help."[22]

Luke Skywalker tried to pull Han Solo into the shared mission to defend the galaxy against the evil Empire, but it takes Han Solo longer than Luke to sacrifice his own life for the liberation of others.

Luke: So. You got your reward and you're just leaving, then?

Han: That's right, yeah. Got some old debts I gotta pay off with this stuff. Even if I didn't, you don't think I'd be fool enough to stick around here, do you? Why don't you come with us? You're pretty good in a fight. We could use you.

Luke: Come on. Why don't you take a look around? You know what's about to happen, what they're up against. They could use a good pilot like you, you're turning your back on them.

Han: What good is a reward if you ain't around to use it? Besides, attacking that battle station is not my idea of courage. It's more like, suicide.

Luke: Okay. Take care of yourself, Han. I guess that's what you're best at, isn't it?[23]

But Luke's loyalty to others (and to a more meaningful mission than self-preservation) eventually converts Han, who returns to save Luke's life in the ultimate battle against the Death Star.

When you consider Luke's devotion to Han and Princess Leia, Sam Gamgee's loyalty to death toward Frodo, and Harry's unbreakable bond with his friends Ron and Hermione, it becomes clear across all three epics that it is love that forges heroes, binds fellowships, inspires sacrifice, and defeats death. Obi-Wan warns the evil Darth Vader not to kill him because death cannot destroy the existence of love, and resurrection will follow the end of any person's life. He says to Darth Vader, "If you strike me down, I shall become more powerful than you can possibly imagine."[24] These are similar words that Luke speaks at the end of his life to Han Solo's corrupt son Ren. Luke tried to warn him that ultimately evil can never defeat goodness, light, and love.

> Ren: Did you come back to say you forgive me? To save my soul?
> Luke: No. . . . I failed you, Ren. I'm sorry.
> Ren: I'm sure you are! The Resistance is dead! The war is over! And when I kill you, I will have killed the last Jedi!
> Luke: Amazing. Every word of what you just said was wrong. The Rebellion is reborn today. The war is just beginning. And I will not be the last Jedi.[25]

Gandalf speaks to Frodo with kinder but similar words:

> Some believe it is only great power that can hold evil in check, but that is not what I have found. It is the small

everyday deeds of ordinary folk that keep the darkness at bay. Small acts of kindness and love.[26]

Voldemort tries to convince Dumbledore that evil magic is the most powerful force in the world, far more powerful than acts of kindness and love:

> "The old argument," Voldemort said softly. "But nothing I have seen in the world has supported your famous pronouncement that love is more powerful than my kind of magic, Dumbledore." "Perhaps you have been looking in the wrong places," suggested Dumbledore.[27]

Remember that Dumbledore told Harry about the power of love at the end of his first year at Hogwarts when he said,

> If there is one thing Voldemort cannot understand, it is love. He didn't realize that love as powerful as your mother's for you leaves its own mark. Not a scar, no visible sign . . . to have been loved so deeply, even though the person who loved us is gone, will give us some protection forever.[28]

Dumbledore's words echo a phrase spoken by the warrior Elf Haldir, speaking of the ultimate power of love over loss and resurrection over death:

> The world is indeed full of peril and in it there are many dark places. But still there is much that is fair. And though in all lands, love is now mingled with grief, it still grows, perhaps, the greater.[29]

Shortly before his death, Dumbledore tries to explain to Harry why Voldemort cannot kill him and, ultimately, why no dark magic will ever win the wars of the world.

> There is a room in the Department of Mysteries that is kept locked at all times. It contains a force that is at once more wonderful and more terrible than death, than human intelligence, than the forces of nature. It is also, perhaps, the most mysterious of the many subjects for study that reside there. It is the power held within that room that you possess in such quantities and which Voldemort has not at all. That power took you to save Sirius tonight. That power also saved you from possession by Voldemort, because he could not bear to reside in a body so full of the force he detests. In the end, it mattered not that you could not close your mind. It was your heart that saved you.[30]

Is Your Evangelism Epic?

We learn from these contemporary, compelling, and contagious cultural narratives that there are at least four elements to an epic story that grip the listener or reader and challenge them to change or grow or thrive. These elements are a clear call, a meaningful mission, a committed community, and a defined destiny. In my experience, epic evangelism that inspires others to see, know, serve, and love God share these four elements. Theologically, we have our own words for these parts of loving and liberating evangelism. We speak about having a spiritual anthropology, a missiology, an ecclesiology, and an eschatology. These are big words but they express the same core truths as call, mission, community, and destiny. It has been my experience that if you build your understanding and practice of evangelism based on these four ideas, you will experience the inspiring power of epic evangelism.

Is your evangelism epic? If you answer "yes" to most or all of these next four questions, you are well on your way to the kind of belief system that will fuel and fire up your witness of Christ to a broken world. If you are an extrovert, you will do many of these things by talking, praying, or working with others. If you are more of an introvert, you will do more of these things through actions, listening, praying, writing, and offering your presence and patience to the world. No matter who God has made you and is making you to be, I challenge you to inwardly digest these four questions and find ways to outwardly experiment with living an epic discipleship of Jesus Christ. The world is watching and longing for the epic love of God.

Do you know how to communicate clearly (in deeds and/or words) that God is calling the person in front of you, just as God is calling you, into a personal relationship with God that will last and grow beyond death?

Theologians call any perspective on humanity a theological anthropology, a belief about human nature and how God relates to humans. Episcopalians believe that all people are created by God to enter into a relationship with God, by choice, forever. We believe that from conception, God is calling every creature into relationship through love. No one is un-called by God's love.

God knows how many hairs are on our heads (Luke 12:7–9), which is a beautiful image to say that God knows us better than we know ourselves. We are known and we are called to accept and deepen a relationship with God that is both deeply personal and powerfully communal in the body of the church. Every life has a unique purpose in God's creation and every life has meaning because God's unconditional and sacrificial love establishes the priceless worth of every creature. Epic evangelists find ways to help people see, hear, and believe the meaning and purpose in every life. Epic evangelists listen and love people into an awareness that God is calling their name and their life into love, redemption, and joy.[31]

Do you know how to communicate clearly (in deeds and/or words) that God has a mission to love all creation that includes every human life and it is worthy to make choices and sacrifices to join?

Theologians call this idea missiology, the belief that God has a mission to love the whole world into a new heaven and a new earth, bringing justice, redemption, and peace on earth as it is in heaven. Epic evangelists have accepted this invitation themselves to join God's mission to love the world into redemption through Jesus Christ and the power of the Holy Spirit. We understand that Jesus did not come to earth to condemn the world, but to save it, and so with deeds and words we share God's invitation to join God in loving the world into eternal life by renouncing evil and darkness and living as a child of Christ's light.[32]

Can you explain (with deeds and/or words) that following Jesus in the world is to join a community on an epic journey together, together accomplishing miracles that one could never witness or achieve alone?

This is what we call our ecclesiology, our view that the individual followers of Jesus, through baptism, become one Body and one Church. Galatians 2:20 says, "It is no longer I who live, but it is Christ who lives in me. And the life I now live in the flesh I live by faith in the Son of God, who loved me and gave himself for me." Members of the body of Christ no longer live separate lives from other followers of Christ. We are connected to one another as siblings in Christ forever. Epic evangelists communicate this Good News to the world: in baptism individual lives are bound together in the waters of baptism. In Christ, we are new creations and we are children in one family and members of the Trinity through Christ. Epic evangelists proclaim to the world: there is no such thing as being alone.[33]

Can you describe in deeds and words your confidence that in the end, love wins?

Theologians call the future eschatology, which comes from the Greek word *eschaton*, meaning "end" or "goal." Epic evangelists can maintain hope and even joy in the face of immense suffering in their lives and in the world because they know how the story of creation ends. No matter how broken, how tragic, or how unjust any chapter of any person's or the whole world's story unfolds, it is the radical and audacious belief of the epic evangelist that no chapter of darkness or pain can change the ultimate ending of the story of creation. Although the story of the world unfolds like a frustrating mystery mixed with pain and beauty, we believe that death in all its forms of illness, division, depression, or decay has been defeated. No one and nothing can stop the world from moving toward redemption and new creation, despite the horrific potential for pain and loss in the human condition. It can be a struggle for a disciple or a scandal to a skeptic to continue to believe in the ultimate recreation of the world into a new heaven and a new earth, but the epic evangelist holds to this view that all promises of God "are yes in Christ." Followers of Jesus believe that death has lost its sting because it has been defeated by Christ on the cross, even if this is the only light we hold in the valleys and shadows of death around us. Hebrews 2:8–9 begins to explain the tension in which we live, gripping the hope of resurrection amidst a world that wrestles with death:

> Now in subjecting all things to them, God left nothing outside their control. As it is, we do not yet see everything in subjection to them, but we do see Jesus, who for a little while was made lower than the angels, now crowned with glory and honor because of the suffering of death, so that by the grace of God he might taste death for everyone.

An epic evangelist learns to hold on to hope—through prayer, fellowship, liturgy, and sacrament—in the freedom from death in all its forms earned on the Cross. Epic hope is a practice of trusting that the resurrection will empty every tomb.

Conclusion: Be That Building

In the first year or two of my high school teaching career, I received (what I believed at the time to be) an incredible offer from my administrators for the school's spring break holiday. I was offered an all-expenses paid, twelve-day trip to multiple countries in Europe with a huge stipend—if I would serve as a chaperone for a student trip. I was young and inexperienced enough to think this was a great deal. It did not occur to me at the time to ask why older and more seasoned colleagues of mine "would not touch" the offer. So I and four other naïve teachers led a World War II history trip for thirty-five high school students. I have never counted to thirty-five so many times, nor was there ever a more frightening number than thirty-four.

Our itinerary was to start in France, beginning on the beaches of Normandy. We went on to Paris, then to London, and eventually ended in Germany. At every stop we had wonderful lodging, flawless transportation, and local tour guides with advanced degrees in history, architecture, and political science. On paper, it was a perfectly planned immersion in twentieth-century history. In reality, these fifteen- and sixteen-year-olds were more interested in their own social dynamics than anything said by a tour guide or teacher about European history. Oh sure, there were a handful of students who thrived in the immersive educational experience, asking questions at every turn, taking pictures and notes at every stop of the journey. But the vast majority of students were focused on the gossip of the hour, who was dating whom, if they could sneak alcohol past their chaperones, smoke behind the hotel, or sneak into each other's rooms after curfew. There was little or no malice among the students, either for their chaperones or their peers, and most of the students had a truly enjoyable and memorable time.

However, it was difficult to puncture their personal dramas and social goals. Europe was a nearly mute backdrop to the daily chronicles of their social cliques. The group was large enough to be a microcosm of any high school divided into the classic subcultures of high school life: "cool kids," marginal and socially awkward kids, drama club kids, poor kids, ache-ridden quiet kids, bombastic immature kids, and the handful of true troublemakers that thirst for the kinds of risks that keep chaperones up at night. My role was to break through the patterns of exclusion, hazing, and bullying that are too common in adolescence. The classic book on the darkness of human nature, *Lord of the Flies,* was probably written by a high school chaperone.

My idealism at that time in my teaching career led me daily, if not hourly, to try and rescue the humanity of my students on this trip. I tried to reward students with attention, even prizes of food or extra free time for any signs of investment in learning about history. I tried to inspire them to learn alongside their desire to play with history trivia games or tirelessly planned scavenger hunts. To break into the cruel cliques that too often excluded others, I assigned bus seats, dictated roommate pairings, and set up seating charts for meals. But my social engineering was mostly unsuccessful and even resented. There were tears from someone nearly every day in response to an act of meanness, exclusion, or breaking rules. For those who did not cry, there were nonetheless signs of acting out and destructive behavior. There were times when I forgot what country we were in, so focused was I on whatever drama of the hour was unfolding. As the leader of the trip I felt the heavy burden of making sure that as many students as possible learned something, avoided danger, and arrived home not too hurt by other students. I slept for almost two entire days when we got home.

A visit to the Dachau concentration camp in Germany was on the last day. Looking back, we should have never ended a twelve-day trip at such a significant and impactful place. After ten days of travel, both students and adults were exhausted in every way and longing to go home. Visiting a World War II death camp would require more mental and spiritual energy and fortitude than we could muster.

The bus ride to the camp was the quietest our group had been in eleven days. Our tour guide gave a short speech at the hotel before we left, explaining the significance of visiting a concentration camp and warning students of the potential triggers or trauma that the trip might stir. This declaration hit the students hard. For the first time, I felt that they put their own socializing to the side as they appeared ready to look up and look out around them, albeit caused by fear of the unknown. More than one student quietly started to cry as our bus bumped and rocked as it drove over the stony ground and through the iron gate entrance of Dachau. I was teary, too.

Dachau was the first concentration camp set up by the Nazis, primarily for political prisoners and other dissidents against Hitler. Eventually, it took in mainly Jewish prisoners, killing thousands and thousands in its crematoriums. The tour was devastating. Some students retreated to their phones or skipped exhibits, most were simply crushed and silenced by the experience. Tears. Silence. And occasionally as we walked by the ovens or the crowded prison cells, quiet gasps. What I can still remember is that their eyes were open so wide. I had not noticed the eyes of my students for eleven days, but as we were led through the hell of that death camp, I felt like all I could see on their faces were their terrified eyes opened so wide I could see all the white around each soulful center of brown or blue. Despite eleven days of periodic frustration with nearly all of them, at that hour I wanted only to hug them all. And most looked like they wanted to be held as well.

We all agreed to end the day by meeting up at the exit of the camp when all the touring was over. I hoped this freedom to choose one's pace in walking through the large camp would give each student the freedom to take their time and have only one requirement of the day: to meet at a fixed time and place before we left for the airport. Admittedly, I was also creating space for myself to take in the experience without interruption or even conversation until the end. I had never been to anything as horrible as this in my life.

Holy Space

Uniquely, Dachau was the camp where religious leaders who taught or preached against the Nazi party were sent. More religious leaders were murdered there than at any other camp. As a result, when the camp was being prepared to open to the public, small plots of land in an open field were given over to different Christian denominations so that they could build small memorials, chapels, or churches in remembrance of their leaders who died. There is a small Catholic convent in this section of religious structures where Carmelite nuns have taken vows for life to live behind the high walls and gates of the tiny cloistered building and pray for peace in the world.

All of these small structures and little churches line the edges of the gravel path that leads to the exit of the camp. It is the last area visitors walk through before leaving. Around the time our group was set to meet up, I made my way along this road of memorials. I was beginning to transition my heart from personal sadness and learning to taking up my role again as the adult leader of our large group. I looked around the large field of religious structures near the exit but did not see many of our students. There were only about four or five boys, pacing silently in circles near the gate. I was intentionally one of the last people in our group's two-hour path through the camp. I stayed at the back of the group for most of the day so that we didn't lose sight or awareness of any students who might be sad or need support. As the caboose of the group, I couldn't figure out where most of the students were. I started to wonder, even getting mad at them in my head. Were most of them off in some secret side area, laughing or on their phones or being disrespectful? My pace picked up and my eyes were darting in every direction. How do you lose about thirty kids? And what level of trouble or offensive behavior had they chosen in this most sacred burial ground? My anger was boiling at a new fever point. I think I even stewed out loud, "Bending rules again, even in a concentration camp . . . is there nothing sacred?"

I walked past the largest religious memorial, a church building. I noticed two of my students near the entrance. I walked up to them and asked where the others were. The two girls pointed at the church. "Just about everyone is still in there." I found this statement immediately puzzling. This group was always so fractured into smaller cliques, from the moment we left the airport. We were only an "everyone" on this trip in buses or at tables to eat. What could be inside this building that my students wanted to see?

The two girls walked away toward the bus before they could tell me how to get into the church. There was no entrance that I could find on the ground level. I could see that it was built mostly underground so as not to overpower the size of the other smaller memorials along the gravel road. All I could see was a ramp from the ground level that wrapped around the building, making a spiral pathway down into an entrance ten or twelve feet below the ground. I made my way quickly down the ramp.

As soon as I opened the door, I could hear a hum of familiar voices. Called the Church of Reconciliation, it was built by the international Presbyterian Church to memorialize Presbyterians who died in the camp as well as a gift to any person wanting a quiet and safe space to process their experience of the camp in a holy place. Although the voices of my students were familiar, I felt strange. The church was very dark and tomb-like. There were few windows and only one door to enter or leave. The church was one room. There was a small wooden table at the front; some might call it an altar but there was nothing formal or ornate about it. There was only one cross in the whole room, maybe a foot high and wide, carved into a copper plate and hanging somewhat crooked and uncentered on a wall. There was no other art. The walls were uneven stone. There were about six short benches, each a slightly different height. Most of the floor space was uneven stone. I can't remember any colors at all.

The shape of the sanctuary room was odd. The room had four walls, but each wall was a different length and even a different height. The seam line of the ceiling and walls was very uneven.

Was this design meant to be a cave? I wasn't even sure where to look to understand the space. My initial reaction was that the architect had failed at anything one would call beauty or even meaning. I felt guilty about the words that floated through my head to describe what I was seeing: sloppy, dusty, unserious, and unkempt.

All these impressions formed in blink of an eye. And in their wake, my eyes fell on my students spread around the odd room. Quickly embarrassed and angry, I saw my kids spread out on the floor, sitting cross-legged and talking as if it were a café. A few students were lying down on the uneven benches, as if they were sleeping in a bus station. I heard quiet words, stories being told, and even a hint of occasional levity in laughter. Boys were stretched out with their heads in the laps of girls—not obscene or even sexual, but overt connection and care. Girls were quietly talking while braiding hair. Everything they were doing was hushed but human in every way. You would not guess they had all just walked for hours through a relentless presentation of raw evidence of the most demonic dimensions of human choice and power, as well as hearing hints of millions of stories of enduring human survival. They seemed, in a word, okay.

Resurrection

I was still embarrassed by the sheer casualness of the group. I walked toward them to whisper loudly that they ought to sit up, stop braiding hair, stop cuddling and for the love of God, stop smiling so much in their storytelling and bonding. On my way to giving my lecture on decorum, I passed a pile of papers on a bench left for visitors and meant to orient people to the space. I picked one up and glanced at it, hoping to learn something quickly about the architecture and its intention. I was hoping I could quote something from that handout to use in correction of the students who were treating this sanctuary like someone's basement playroom back home. I have kept that worn piece of paper for twenty years and I will never forget its two paragraphs, written in German and English, welcoming visitors to the space:

Dear Visitor,

Welcome to the Church of Reconciliation. At first sight, maybe this church seems to be very cold, grey, and dark. Many visitors have this first impression. However, when you take a closer look, its distinctive architecture begins to speak. There are two specific design characteristics which can be distinguished in this building. One is the absence of right angles. This, in an area which is determined by right-angled things. The camp, the inspection place, the flogging table, all foundations, everything is right angled . . . The architect thought the fact that everything had right angles to be a sheer symbol of the National Socialist murder system. Heinrich Mann once spoke about the "exactness within the loathsome." The architectural design of the Church of Reconciliation is meant to be a contrast to all right-angled things of terror.

The second characteristic is that the church is built like a path, leading slowly into the depths. Depth—a symbol of suffering and death, but also of contradiction and resistance. Also, a symbol of shame, as if you wished the ground would swallow you up . . . What is important is that an awareness of depth does not destroy. From the depths, a human can moan, cry, shout, or pray. "Out of the depths I cry to you, O God . . . ." Psalm 130

The information page concluded by saying that walking up the ramp as you leave is meant to be an experience of physical resurrection. The building was constructed to walk you through the soul's experience of the camp again, but this time within its consecrated walls and embraced by its gospel hope. Its planners wanted visitors to actually descend to the dark depths of earth as a ritual that the camp forces you to do. But in that place, we become terrified at the horror humans can bring about. Anyone with a conscience might be trapped or suffocated by the truth and presence of evil in the world and in the human heart. One could leave Dachau in the depths of depression, but these church builders wanted to offer a final experience of depth bathed and blessed in Christian hope. Their offering to humanity was an experience that brings your physical body down and then up, into the dark and then ascending into the light of day.

I looked up from the page and saw my students with new eyes. None of them had this piece of paper or had even noticed the pile from which it came. But of course, they had found comfort here. Their souls were battered by exposure to a death camp, but in this space—a space intentionally designed to soothe the terror and trauma of evil and invite the soul to light and life—they did not experience judgment or rules or conformity.

I then noticed that they were mostly huddled as one group. Students who had not spoken to each other at all on this trip were sitting face to face. Students who had not touched anyone for ten days were giving or getting back rubs. Girls and boys were mixed with more stillness than angst. Kids in different grades were sharing stories and listening—actually listening—to one another. I do not want to over-generalize or over-romanticize the moment. But in a word, the architecture was . . . working.

I began this book by stating that "evangelism is listening." And the builders of the Church of Reconciliation created a building that listens to its visitors and responds directly, spiritually, curiously, compassionately, and physically to their deepest wounds and sense of wonder. Countless details of the sanctuary were planned and carved in response to a process of discernment by the planners to delve into the questions and scars the Dachau camp might raise or cause in human beings. The goal of the building is clear: communicate the resurrection in a place of death. But their discernment was not just to meet the longings of visitors. Clearly, there was deep discernment on the patterns and crimes of the Nazi worldview.

People had clearly studied how evil had functioned and what levels and angles were used to pervert beauty, to violate justice, to convert the good into evil, to oppress, and to terrorize. These builders knew the depth of depravity of the world and that knowledge made them fluent in the experiences of people hurt by that evil. This knowledge builds credibility and proves devotion to the visitor. The building whispers, "I know what you have seen and I know what that evil is about." Intimacy is built between building and any bruised soul that enters it because the contrasting shape of the building is a sign that its worldview is opposed to the calculating nature of mass murder.

The lesson of this church in the concentration camp is not that all our buildings—or all our speech or techniques as evangelists—need to be dark or without right angles. The grace of God taught in this death camp is an example of "evangelism"— the longings of people who enter it and find a way to communicate the gospel—the literal experience of being resurrected—into that particular experience.

Pentecost Today

Communication of the gospel can happen in a variety of ways. A simple example are churches that set up water fountains along the routes of marathons or put drinking fountains in dog parks. The wisdom is to seek and know the longings of others which we believe are forged deep in the person by God. Once we stop and listen to others and to the world deeply enough, we can know to communicate the gospel in terms that are natural to the seeker.

In the Acts of the Apostles 2:1–13, we find the story of Pentecost. All too often people remember this story vaguely as a time when a few of the followers of Jesus gathered, spoke about God, and then all those around them from dozens of other nations understood the Aramaic-speaking apostles. But pay close attention to that miracle. What happened on that day was not that those foreigners were given the miraculous gift of understanding the language of the disciples. The miracle was that the disciples were given the gift to speak the languages of the seekers surrounding them. The Church was, by a miracle, made fluent in the culture and languages surrounding her, not the other way around. The message of Pentecost is that the call of the Church is not to hope and pray that one day the world understands us. Rather, it is our mission to ask God for help in learning and speaking the gospel into the languages of the seekers of the world. We are called to fluency in the language and life of the seeker in order to share with them the story of Jesus Christ.

I saw a building break down the chosen and cherished walls between teenagers with just a few simple signs and symbols of acceptance and embrace. I saw a building meet its visitors in the depths of their doubt that humans could ever love or be loved and give them a literal pathway out of death's depths to light and life on the earth. A sanctuary as sparse and simple as the lowly manger, the empty tomb, or the upper room stands open as a crèche for the soul and place of incarnation.

As an evangelist, I want to be that building. I want to seek and learn and know the suffering and the dreams of those God puts in front of me. I want my life to be stable enough for people to feel safe to enter it. I want to be open enough to have room for any kind of person. I want to be humble enough to let others feel deep sorrow in my presence and feel sure that I am not afraid to meet them there. I want to have ramps in my imagination that walk me and those I meet upward toward light and love and hope. I want to ignore the rigid rules that reign in religion or any culture that cuts out the odd and pushes otherness to the margins. I want more curves in my curiosity and fewer right angles in my assumptions. I want my face to be a place where people let go and start to talk and listen and touch and heal. I want to stand in camps of death and be a sanctuary of life. I want the shape of my life and not just the script of my speech to proclaim the resurrection of Christ.

Are you willing to go and plant yourself in the camps of death in the world and sculpt your life to show and share the gospel of Christ with the souls of others? That is my daily prayer for me and for you.

Notes

1 Linda Mercadante, *Belief Without Borders* (New York: Oxford University Press, 2014), 1.

2 Ibid., 2.

3 *Book of Occasional Services 2003* (New York: Church Pension Fund, 2004), 176.

4 Ibid., 186.

5 *The New Catechism of the Catholic Church* (Boston: Pauline Press, 1992), 436.

6 Mercadante, *Belief Without Borders,* 251–253.

7 Rowan Williams, "God's Mission and Ours in the 21st Century," an address by the Archbishop of Canterbury to a meeting of the Intercontinental Church Society at Lambeth Palace, June 2009.

8 C.S. Lewis, *Surprised by Joy* (New York: Harcourt Brace Jovanovich, 1984), 115.

9 "Likewise the Spirit helps us in our weakness; for we do not know how to pray as we ought, but that very Spirit intercedes with sighs too deep for words" (Romans 8:26).

10 C.S. Lewis, *Mere Christianity* (New York: Collier Books, 1980), 32–33.

11 J.R.R. Tolkien, "Fairy Stories" in *Tree and Leaf* (New York: HarperCollins, 2001).

12 J.K. Rowling, *Harry Potter and the Sorcerer's Stone* (New York: Scholastic, 1997), 50.

13 *Star Wars: Episode IV—A New Hope* [motion picture]. United States: George Lucas, 1977.

14 Ibid.

15 J.R.R. Tolkien, *The Fellowship of the Ring* (New York: Houghton Mifflin, 1994), 264.

16 Peter Jackson, Barrie M. Osborne, Fran Walsh, and Tim Sanders (producers); Peter Jackson (director), *The Lord of the Rings: The Fellowship of the Ring* [motion picture]. USA: New Line Cinema, 2001.

17 Tolkien, *The Fellowship of the Ring*, 262.

18 Chris Columbus, David Heyman, and Mark Radcliffe (producers); Steve Kloves (screenwriter); Alfonso Cuarón (director), *Harry Potter and the Order of the Phoenix* [motion picture]. Burbank, CA: Warner Home Video, 2007. Warner Bros; 1492 Pictures; Heyday Films.

19 Peter Jackson, Barrie M. Osborne, and Fran Walsh (producers); Peter Jackson, (director), *The Lord of the Rings: The Two Towers* [motion picture]. USA: New Line Cinema, 2002.

20 Peter Jackson, Barrie M. Osborne, and Fran Walsh (producers); Peter Jackson (director), *The Lord of the Rings: The Return of the King* [motion picture]. USA: New Line Cinema, 2003.

21 *Harry Potter and the Order of the Phoenix* [motion picture].

22 J.K. Rowling, *Harry Potter and the Order of the Phoenix* (New York: Scholastic, 2003), 761.

23 *Star Wars: Episode IV—A New Hope* [motion picture].

24 Ibid.

25 *Star Wars: Episode VIII—The Last Jedi* [motion picture]. United States: George Lucas, 2017.

26 Carolynne Cunningham and others (producers); Fran Walsh and others (screenwriters); Peter Jackson (director), *"The Hobbit: An Unexpected Journey"* [motion picture] Burbank, CA: Warner Home Video, 2013. A New Line Cinema; Metro-Goldwyn-Mayer Pictures; a Wingnut Films production.

27 J.K. Rowling, *Harry Potter and the Half Blood Prince* (New York: Scholastic, 2005), 444, 445.

28 J.K. Rowling, *Harry Potter and the Philosopher's Stone* (New York: Scholastic, 1997), 299.

29 Tolkien, *The Fellowship of the Ring*, 339.

30 Rowling, *Harry Potter and the Order of the Phoenix*, 843–844.

31 Read the Baptismal Covenant on pages 304–305 of the Book of Common Prayer for helpful language.

32 Read the sections on "The Church," "Holy Baptism," and "The Christian Hope" found in an Outline of the Faith, known as the Catechism found in the Book of Common Prayer.

33 Read The Lord's Prayer and take note that we begin with "Our" and not "My" Father. Read the section of the Catechism on the "The Christian Hope" and the communion of Saints in the Book of Common Prayer on pages 861–862.